The God Diaries

Janice Harris

ABOOKS
Alive Book Publishing

Additional copies may be ordered from the publisher for educational,
business, promotional or premium use.
For information, contact ALIVE Book Publishing at:
alivebookpublishing.com, or call (925) 837-7303.

Book Design by Alex Johnson
Quotes from the Bible are from the New International Version (NIV).

ISBN 13
978-1-63132-178-8

Library of Congress Control Number: 2022917772

Library of Congress Cataloging-in-Publication Data
is available upon request.

First Edition

Published in the United States of America by ALIVE Book Publishing
an imprint of Advanced Publishing LLC
3200 A Danville Blvd., Suite 204, Alamo, California 94507
alivebookpublishing.com

PRINTED IN THE UNITED STATES OF AMERICA

10 9 8 7 6 5 4 3 2 1

Introduction

When my husband was confronted with a chronic, life-threatening illness, I was quite disillusioned by the response of our church community. During the pandemic, when feeling isolated and alone in my suffering, I was directed to strengthen my spiritual life through prayer and meditation on the Word. I began writing down these prayers and insights and, in so doing, was amazed to discover that an authentic fellowship built up around me.

I maintain a strong faith and am a member of a community that grows daily, however, I do not associate myself with any church or religious body. This book is for anyone who wants to explore how the Bible can maintain daily relevance in the modern world. It chronicles my own transition from relying on church to achieving my own, personal connection to the spiritual world.

January 1

"In the beginning God created the heavens and the earth. Now the earth was formless and empty, darkness was on the face of the deep and the Spirit of God was hovering over the waters. And God said, 'Let there be light,' and there was light.'" Genesis 1:1-3

Dear Lord,

Enter my heart and reveal your truth to me. I am wanting to come into contact with my personal inner truth shared only between you and I. I was feeling conflicted yesterday, very conflicted. I had a strong inclination to phone an acquaintance and vent, however, instead I will work on taking my troubles to you. I will learn to sit with my unrest and wait for you to shine your light on the darkness of my soul. I have an intuition that if I continue to do that, your truth will come. I believe also that I will draw to myself other seekers, others who are of a similar mindset and that we will be able to communicate on a different level than I am currently experiencing. I had a fleeting sense of that happening in an exchange that I had yesterday with a fellow traveler so please bring more such exchanges into the realm of my experience.

Amen

January 2

"In the beginning was the Word, and the Word was with God, and the Word was God." John 1:1

Dear Lord,

Last night I had a nightmare. I dreamt that I was drinking and carrying on. I was reliving bits and pieces of a sordid past. I was with my husband and teenaged son and we were out to dinner; I was scantily dressed. I was lying and keeping secrets from them. My husband led us into a building. As soon as we got into the building, my husband and son disappeared. As they disappeared, I realized that we were in a church.

There was a preacher up front and all of the attendees were walking in a procession toward him. I fell down and had a hard time getting up. As I moved closer to the front, I realized that the preacher was reading off names in the book of life. People lined up on two sides based on their eternal destination. I awoke in a sweat realizing that decisions I was making in my life were taking me down the wrong path.

I will seek your Word, Oh Lord, to guide me back to the light. I will pray on my knees each morning. I will listen for your guidance. I will diligently seek the written Word as light for my path. Perhaps I appear on the outside as though I am a devoted Christian. However, you know my heart. You have spoken.

Amen

January 3

"Finally, be strong in the Lord and in his mighty power. Put on the full armor of God, so that you can take your stand against the devil's schemes." Ephesians 6:10-11

Dear Lord,

I am not immune to temptation. Not one of us is. The things that work against me to chink my armor morph or become stronger over time. What I am vulnerable to now may be different than what I was vulnerable to 10 years ago. Similarly, 10 years from now my vulnerabilities will be different than what they are today. Please dear Lord, help me to be able to invite you fully into my heart to strengthen me against my enemies. Please help me to increase my awareness of my imperfections so that I may not be caught off guard.

I desire to feed myself more on your Word. I invite a genuine faith community to surround me so as to be less vulnerable. At the same time however, please help me to allow my heart to remain open to the pain of the world. I do not want to remain cloistered in safety, but to breathe light into darkened souls. Please help me to be able to do that, Oh Lord, without allowing my own light to dim.

You are a divine provider of life and purpose. Please avail yourself to me and to all of my fellow seekers.

Amen

January 4

"...For all who exalt themselves will be humbled, and those who humble themselves will be exalted." Luke 18:14

Dear Lord,

Please help me to be willing to surrender my ego to you today. Thank you for allowing me to be vulnerable and for hearing the whispers of my soul as I pour my heart out to you. Thank you for the handful of intimate friends who are coming into my life and who lovingly offer correction when needed. Help me always to be willing to make time for you so that I may hear your still, small voice inside myself as it guides me.

It is easy to allow the noise of the world into my heart, mind, body and soul. Even with rigorous prayer and meditation the noise can sometimes get through. Throughout my life, when I have allowed my ego to become inflated, you have always humbled me. Please help me to be strong enough to feel the pain of the world; to process it, surrender it and allow it. When I am able to do that, I am able to invite the joy of your healing and unfailing love.

Amen

January 5

"Come to me, all who are weary and burdened, and I will give you rest." Take my yoke upon you and learn from me, for I am gentle and humble in heart, and you will find rest for your souls." Matthew 11: 28-29

Dear Lord,

Please help me to be willing to open my heart and mind to your light. My soul is heavy and filled up with the pain of the world. Please provide me with the rest and comfort that only you can provide. I can be stubborn Oh Lord. I resist your guidance at times and try to take back control. I know that that is not your way.

Please humble my heart, Oh Lord, and make me a channel of your love. Please help me to be able to provide comfort to the distressed. Make me a beacon of your light. So many are hurting now. I trust that there is freedom in your love. Help me to keep my sights always fixed on you. Please provide insight when temptation besieges me. I am weak though you can do all things. Gracious is your name.

Amen

January 6

"For his anger lasts only a moment, But his favor lasts a lifetime, weeping may stay for a night but rejoicing comes in the morning." Psalms 30:5

Dear Lord,

You have blessed me with another day. Please help me to maintain my willingness to do your will. I desire to be of service to all of humankind. I carry the trouble of the world with me, Oh Lord. I devote this time to you today to open myself to your loving care. The light of a new day is your promise of hope.

Today I can breathe, I can feel my heartbeat, I can move about, and I can dream. I can dream of a time when I can share my love and devotion to you with a starving world. I can dream of becoming enveloped in a diverse community of mutual love and support. These are waking dreams that must be brought to life as a creation in you. I will continue to praise you on this blessed journey of life as I embark on my path to truth; a truth you have for everyone.

Amen

January 7

"but few things are needed – or indeed only one." Luke 10:42

Dear Lord,

I have all I need in you. If I keep my eyes focused on you, you bring all I need into my life. You deliver the provisions and the community that suits my needs, if I can only honestly lay myself at your feet. Please help me to be willing today to trust in your abilities and not my own willpower. My ego tends to scheme and plan how I can lie, cheat and steal to get what I think I want or deserve. If I can simply surrender myself to you and allow you to fill me up with your love, I attract all I need to thrive and to provide for those in my circle of influence.

Amen

January 8

"Give us aid against our enemy, for human help is worthless." Psalm 108:12

Dear Lord,

Of myself I am nothing. When I am operating from a place of selfishness, I have no defense against the forces in the world that work against me. It is only through a daily connection with you that I can navigate amidst the dark forces that present themselves as I fight my daily battles. I do rely on wise counsel at times, however, please help me to always use discernment in proceeding with decisions. There are many deceptions that contort your truth and confuse me. I am weak. My only strength comes through you and the glorious community that you are building up around me.

Amen

January 9

"'He will wipe every tear from their eyes. There will be no more death or crying or pain, for the old order of things has passed away." Revelation 21:10

Dear Lord,

My heart has been heavy with the pain of this world. There is sickness, suffering and emotional pain. These bring great suffering to those who choose to awaken. Please help me to always be mindful that following in your ways brings deliverance in the end. Please help me to be able to rest in that assurance. When my heart feels heavy and the tears fall, you are my constant companion.

You hear the whispering of my soul without judgment and provide your gentle hand of guidance, if only I open my heart to hearing your voice. I've discovered that your voice becomes louder and more stern the further I wander off course, in much the same way as, a parent becomes frightened when a child strays too far into the wilderness. Please Lord, help me to always listen and attend to your guidance when I have spiritual unrest, sleep disturbance, an unbalanced diet or other warning signs that I am veering off course.

Lord, I want to get to the finish line. I want your comfort and deliverance from my pain. Please help me to keep my eyes fixed on you today, ever moving onward toward the ultimate goal.

Amen

January 10

"Consider it pure joy, my brothers and sisters, whenever you face trials of many kinds, because you know the testing of faith produces perseverance." James 1:2-3

Dear Lord,

You know the deep whisperings of my soul. You know that I am not above my own specific set of temptations, as we all have our unique set of weaknesses. Please help me, Oh dear one, to always become willing to learn from my transgressions and to turn them humbly over to your grace so that I may be strengthened in those defective areas. I know I will always maintain my own human imperfections, but as I move through this life, may I continue to gain humble awareness of my weaknesses. As I strengthen my spiritual defenses and fill myself up with the cup of your love I become better able to walk through the fire.

Please help me to be willing to persist on the path and not to give up when I stumble. For each day I prove myself unworthy of your perfection. I rest in the assurance of your perfect love as long as I open my heart to the grace that is available to me each day. I don't deserve your love, yet it awaits me. No one of us deserves your love in our lust, gluttony, greed, pride and selfishness, yet it abounds.

Please help me today to be willing to learn from my mistakes. Help me to anticipate how the world works against me and to properly arm myself with your love.

Amen

January 11

"He made the moon to mark the seasons, and the sun knows when to go down." Psalm 104:19

Dear Lord,

When I feel cast adrift amidst the chaos of the world, I look to your creations in the universe for comfort. The rise and the set of the sun, the ebb and the flow of the tides, the waxing and waning of the moon. All of these provide a hidden order. I can ground myself in the miraculous unfolding of a new flower or the cooing of a newborn baby. The world is reborn anew each morning and all of nature renews and replenishes itself. Only in our humanness do we break down the natural order of your kingdom.

The more we try to fight our own humble place in this world, the more we bring destruction upon it. Please Lord, help me to live more in right alignment with the perfection of your kingdom; to fade from this life into eternity without grasping or fighting is the highest honor. Please help me to align myself with your high kingdom and to know that when the sun sets on my finite life, it will rise again.

Amen

January 12

"I press on toward the goal to win the prize for which God has called me heavenward in Christ Jesus." Philippians 3:14

Dear Lord,

You know my heart, all of the troubles of my soul and my secret desires. You know how I stumble and fight temptation every day. I maintain a complete awareness of the inevitability of my human condition. The primal nature of humankind cannot be ignored. Yet when I stumble, I come to you, heart open in prayer and repentance and request forgiveness. I am driven by a higher calling not to dwell in my primal nature, but to allow you to carry me through to your higher realms.

If I open my heart to you, I can fill my cup with your love. You strengthen me and give me wisdom through prayer and petition. I then become sanctified in you. There is power in prayer for me. There is power in seeking wise counsel. Please help me to keep my eyes always fixed on the prize of your beloved nature and to not let my soul dwell in this world, which will fade away in the blink of an eye.

Amen

January 13

"Keep watch over yourselves and all the flock of which the Holy Spirit has made you overseers." Acts 20:28

Dear Lord,

Please help me to maintain an awareness of my human tendencies to wander off course. Help me to keep daily watch over my dishonesty and thought deception that can lead me astray. Open my heart and level my pride each day so that I may always be willing to seek wise counsel when in times of doubt. My humanness speaks so loudly at times. Each day I fall short in some way, but hopefully I also learn a bit more about myself and how to polish the chinks in my armor.

Please help me to provide a healthy community for others who are seeking. Help me to be able to help build a fellowship for myself of honesty and accountability so that I may always be strengthened in your ways.

Amen

January 14

"'But I tell you, love your enemies and pray for those who persecute you, that you may be children of your Father in heaven.'" Matthew 5:44

Dear Lord,

Please help me to always remember that all people are your loving creation. Please help me to respond in lovingkindness when slighted and not in retaliation and resentment. When I am hurt or angry with another, my inclination is to respond in kind. Lord, I have learned over time that my enemies are my greatest teachers.

They help me to see my own weaknesses and shortcomings. Generally if there is discord in one of my relations, it is because the other party is manifesting qualities that are also true for myself. May I be willing to acknowledge these character weaknesses today, Oh Lord, and to turn from them.

Please help me to open myself to the daily full experience of the blessed life. Pain, discord and disharmony are a part of this fallen world. It is only in continuing to follow in your ways, despite the challenges, that we can know peace.

Amen

January 15

"..'Be still and know that I am God;'" Psalm 46:10

Dear Lord,

Your Word speaks to me this morning through this verse. Please help me to be willing to lay aside my worldly concern and rest in your perfect love. My ego takes over at times and I try to orchestrate and control outcomes. I take back the reins and that weighs heavy on my heart as I begin to feel isolated and alone. Please help me to put my focus today on nurturing my relationship with you.

As I broaden the experience of my morning devotion, your voice becomes clearer. It is less obscured by worldly concerns. There is beginning to be an indwelling that I want to grow. Please help me to always maintain the willingness to make the time for you. Relationships are nurtured in spending time. If I make time each day for your voice to flow in, the knowing becomes clearer. I gain more assurance. For me, daily devotion to prayer and meditation is the only way to open myself up to that still, small voice that whispers inside my soul.

As daily exercise makes strong muscles and builds endurance, the more time I spend with you increases my knowledge and decreases my uncertainty.

Amen

January 16

"'You will seek me and find me when you seek me with all your heart" Jeremiah 29:13

Dear Lord,

I have poured my whole heart out to you. Only you know all of me. You know my exalted aspirations as well as the depths of my transgressions. As I have journeyed through this life, I have stumbled many times. My sins have wounded me deeply and temporarily blocked me off from you. I have endless gratitude for your grace as you continue to hear my heart and my petitions for help.

When I cease hiding in shame and allow myself to trust you to guide me back from the detours I have taken on the road of life, you always avail yourself to me. You are perfect in your love for me. Through each of my transgressions, you have loved me back to wholeness when I continue to seek the goodness of your love.

It is only when I try to hide myself from you that my spiritual growth becomes blocked. You know all of me, Oh Lord and I need to allow the light of your goodness to shine through me into the darkened recesses of my soul.

Amen

January 17

"'For by the grace given me I say to every one of you; Do not think of yourself more highly than you ought, but rather think of yourself with sober judgment, in accordance with the faith that God has distributed to each one of you.'"
Romans 12:3

Dear Lord,

You are a good and gracious Lord. Your Word speaks to me as I open my heart and mind to hear your message. I begin each day with meditation and communicating with you on my knees in prayer. When I humble my heart, as you direct me, I open myself up to receiving you. Please help me to always work to step out of ego and to surrender my desire to control to your goodness.

As I have journeyed through this life, I have experienced many trials and hurts. Many times I have allowed myself to harden in an effort to protect myself. It is only in pouring my heart out to you through intimate petition that I open myself to healing. By embracing your graciousness, I invite fellowship that continues to uplift me in my spiritual growth.

Please Lord, help me to be a beacon of light today to all who are hurting. So many suffer in silence and attempt to mask their pain. We are a fallen people, only made whole again through the goodness of your love.

Amen

January 18

"'If you believe, you will receive whatever you ask for in prayer.'" Matthew 21:22

Dear Lord,

Your goodness abounds. Thank you for opening my heart to hear your voice today. I feel heard and validated in a way I am incapable of describing. When, at first, I embarked upon this journey of devotion through prayer and meditation, I was wounded. I was in a place of deep soul pain and the manner in which I was relating to you was not healthy.

Under the guidance of some trusted fellows, I embarked upon this journey with much resistance. I did so only because I could see your work in their lives in a manner that was not present in my own. I was extremely doubtful and resistant, however, I made a leap of faith and committed to it regardless.

Since that time, I have experienced boundless enrichment in my relationship with you. My life is not without deep, soul pain. You have, however, become my most intimate companion and you carry me through the many trials that present themselves. You bless my life in ways previously unimaginable. My life, which once seemed to me to be falling apart, is now falling into place.

Your love is unfailing. You light my way in the darkness as long as I open my heart and allow it. All glory and honor is yours, Oh Lord.

Amen

January 19

"I will say of the Lord, 'He is my refuge and my fortress, my God in whom I trust.'" Psalm 91:2

Dear Lord,

You are fast becoming my closest confidant. I pour out my heart to you each day and you hear me. You provide light in the darkness and comfort in times of pain. My days are not without their ups and downs. There are victories and defeats. You are the one constant. Through my devotion, you soothe my pain and strengthen me in times of weakness.

As long as I nurture my relationship with you daily and keep that channel open, I know that I can come to you in times of trouble. You nourish me and soothe my soul. You bring others into my life who also seek your comfort and care. You are the great provider, Oh Lord. Please help me always to maintain the willingness to humble myself to you each day. For as I pour myself out, you fill me up and strengthen me.

Amen

January 20

"'Be joyful in hope, patient in affliction, faithful in prayer. Share with the Lord's people who are in need. Practice hospitality." Romans 12:12

Dear Lord,

You are present with me through all aspects of my life. In good times, my gratitude brings joy. In times of suffering I can go to you for comfort. Each day I humble myself to you in prayer so that you may have all of me. You have blessed me with the gift of life and I live in humble service to you and your ways.

You are my lifeline. Your essence breathes life into me on darkened days and allows me to lift others up when I am feeling strong. Your Word speaks to me and helps me to gauge whether I am going in the right direction or not. I also learn when I am needing to make course corrections.

Glory and honor to you, Oh Lord, as you have not abandoned me despite the many ways in which I fall short of your perfect love.

Amen

January 21

"The light shines in the darkness, and the darkness has not overcome it." John 1:5

Dear Lord,

There have been many times throughout my life that I have wandered in the darkness. I have been left feeling as though I have been cast adrift in an endless ocean. When I open my heart to you in prayer and meditation, you provide guidance.

You know all of me. All of my weaknesses and struggles, as I have opened my heart and mind to you. At times I get off course. I close myself off to hearing you. Please help me to always lift my sights upward toward your kingdom and seek to walk the path of kindness. Please help me to constantly seek your navigational beacon and direct my course toward your kingdom.

Amen

January 22

"'for the Holy Spirit will teach you at that time what you should say.'" Luke 12:12

Dear Lord,

Please help me to always be an open channel of your peace and to allow the spirit to speak through me. I can be quite timid and shy, however when moved by your stirrings I find power. The voice of my own ego speaks volumes. When I empty myself of my ego and allow you fully into my heart, mind, body and soul, I can speak your truth and be your witness.

Help me to always remember to turn to you before speaking; to allow you to direct my thoughts, words and actions. Sometimes I have an innate instinct to respond from a bruised ego, which never produces a godly result. It is only through me having a humble heart that the Spirit can fully enter. Please help me to be willing to work daily to achieve and maintain that level of humility. May my speech be uplifting and unifying in a broken and disjointed world.

Amen

January 23

"This is my blood of the covenant, which is poured out for many for the forgiveness of sins." Matthew 26:28

Dear Lord,

Thank you for so selflessly sacrificing yourselves for the betterment of humanity. You were very dedicated and principled. You have freed your believers of sin. To those on that outside of that group, you challenged authority and gave voice to the marginalized. The spirit is alive here on earth and we all may partake of that magic. Let us pause now to invite that in.

We all have our own crosses to bear in this life. Because of how you fortify me each day, I do not have to run from those obstacles or buckle under the pressure. Some days, I feel as though I've reached my breaking point, but your love is unfailing. You continue to provide guidance and direction to me in my hour of need.

You are a good and gracious Lord. You renew me each day and give my life meaning.

Amen

January 24

"'and call on me in the day of trouble; I will deliver you and you will honor me.'" Psalm 50:15

Dear Lord,

Only you know my true heart. You know all of my challenges and struggles. Although my heart belongs to you, I am still vulnerable to becoming ensnared by temptation. I open my heart to you today. I do not keep secrets from you or hide my motives. You walk with me, providing me with strength and guidance.

Oh Lord, the struggles of my human condition are very real. Please help me to always be willing to turn to you first, instead of relying on my own flawed judgment. There is always an open line of communication with you, if I choose it. I invite you into my heart and mind. Please strengthen me against dark forces.

Amen

January 25

"Now faith is confidence in what we hope for and the assurance of what we do not see." Hebrews 11:1

Dear Lord,

You know my true heart. I am not without my own fears and doubts. We would hardly be human without those. However, as I give more of myself over to you each day, gradually you deliver me from my struggles. I am learning to allow you to empower me.

I give you all of me today, Oh Lord. I surrender myself to your will and to the laws of your kingdom. Despite my ego, I know that in doing so, I will be richly rewarded. You have blessed my life thus far in unimaginable ways, despite the various struggles I have had. I summon you this morning to strengthen me in my walk. I know that you are present with us here, when we earnestly seek.

Amen

January 26

"Restore to me the joy of your salvation and grant me a willing spirit to sustain me." Psalm 51:12

Dear Lord,

Today I have physical pain and I feel challenged to muster the strength to get through the day. Your Word sustains me and provides me with guidance. Sometimes I know that you are there, but I don't directly feel your presence and I feel sad.

I want to feel alive again in the joy of your love. I know that if I continue to seek and follow your commands that I will be renewed. You always avail yourself to me in this way when I lay myself earnestly at your feet. You are a good and gracious Lord, worthy of much praise.

Amen

January 27

"I will give thanks to the Lord because of his righteousness;
I will sing praises of the name of the Lord Most High."
Psalm 7:17

Dear Lord,

You are God above all. You guide my life and provide hope in dark days. I am grateful each day for your presence in my life. I am not worthy of your love, yet you continue to walk with me. Your grace is an endless blessing in my life.

Your Word instructs me how to right my path when I veer off course. You provide a community about me in whom I can confide when I don't know which way to turn. You light my path in the darkness. As long as I walk in your way, I have nothing to fear. Please help me to be firm in eliminating sin from my life and not tolerating what I know needs to be blotted out. I am not perfect, by any means, however may I draw nearer to your likeness each day.

Amen

January 28

"Do nothing out of selfish ambition or vain conceit. Rather, in humility value others above yourselves" Philippians 2:3

Dear Lord,

Please help me always to seek to love and serve others above my selfish schemes and overbearing demands. I do need to prioritize myself and take care of myself but only insofar as I can maintain my spiritual wellness. I also need to love and serve others.

Another thing that I have learned is that I cannot be useful if I am not properly caring for myself. If I am not rested and fed myself, both physically and spiritually, I have nothing to give. Please help me to always make my self-care a priority so that I may make the pursuit of service my life's mission.

Glory to you Oh Lord.

Amen

January 29

"Guide me in your truth and teach me, for you are my God and Savior, and my hope is in you all day long." Psalm 25:5

Dear Lord,

I invite you into my heart and mind today. Please fill my spirit with the joy that only you can provide. I wait in joyful hope of the unity that only your kingdom can provide. Although I balk at times, when I am filled with the spirit, you grant me patience and tolerance through trials.

Prayer is my lifeline to you. You hear my heart. You fortify me, fill me up and give me strength. You are gracious in allowing me to enter into communion with you in this way. Your love is beautiful and perfect.

Amen

January 30

"But if we walk in the light, as he is in the light, we have fellowship with one another...." 1 John 1:7

Dear Lord,

When I am living my life in my defective, human condition, with my sinful thoughts and unhealthy habits, I am lonely and isolated. When I make a leap of faith and step into the light of your love, I am surrounded by others who struggle and strive in kind. When I open my heart to you humbly, you bring into my life the exact players I need to carry me through my struggles.

However lonely and isolated my human condition may seem, there are always others struggling in a like manner. When I pour out my fear and doubt to you, you breathe your light into me. I can then carry this light to others to build up a godly fellowship around me. I am a wretched and undeserving soul, yet you fill my cup each day in response to my desperate cries. You comfort me so that I may, in turn, do your bidding in this fallen world.

Amen

January 31

"Submit to one another out of reverence for Christ."
Ephesians 5:21

Dear Lord,

We have become such prideful people here in my Western culture. We have many glorious freedoms from which to construct our own individual personae. While that is an amazing gift of your creation, it can also necessitate a sense of self-reliance that is stifling and hurtful to personal growth.

People need people. We are meant to be communal. Please help me, Lord, to be willing each day to submit my own ego to you so that I may enter into a community with other like-minded folks. I have tried living life on my own terms and it didn't work. It leads to frustration, despair and insanity. Please help me never to discount the importance of having a network of other believers as active participants in my life. Please help me to be willing to be an active participant in the lives of others.

Open my eyes today, Oh Lord. Open my heart and mind to those who want to walk in your way. Humble my heart and bring my true tribe into my life.

Amen

February 1

"....I will pour out my Spirit on all people, Your sons and daughters will prophesy, young men will see visions, old men will dream dreams." Acts 2:17

Dear Lord,

I had a dream last night that I was carrying around dark secrets from the past that I had been concealing. I had simply swept them under the carpet and continued on with my life. Surely we all have our secret primal nature that hides away; a guilty pleasure that we feed when no one is looking.

Please Lord, help me not to spend my energy dwelling in the past. Help me to always come to you with my struggles and to open my heart genuinely to you so that I may hear your voice. May I invite like-minded fellows into my life who are willing to continually do the same. Thank you for how you speak to me. Please help me to continue to leave my heart and mind open to receive your messages.

Amen

February 2

"Let the message of Christ dwell among you richly as you teach and admonish one another with wisdom through psalms, hymns and songs from the Spirit, singing to God with gratitude in your hearts." Colossians 3:16

Dear Lord,

Please help me to pour out my true heart honestly to my fellows. Humble my heart so that I may always respond to correction and guidance. I come to you in gratitude today as you have richly blessed me with a trusted inner circle of confidants who can hear the troubles of my heart.

It is easy to find myself lost in the messages of the world. My fellows, along with my daily connection to you, help me to navigate the difficult terrain of life. I can easily recognize members of my soul-tribe today whereas I have spent many years in the past trying to force myself into a mold that didn't fit. You help me to know my true heart; to nourish the gifts you have provided me. Although I know I will always remain imperfectly human, please help me to continue to maintain the willingness to grow in your likeness each day.

Amen

February 3

"Therefore confess your sins to each other and pray for each other so that you may be healed. The prayer of a righteous person is powerful and effective." James 5:16

Dear Lord,

Help me to keep nothing from you today. My sins hide in the dark but when brought into the light, my heart is opened and I may be healed from the errors of my ways. I have a tendency at times to veer off course. Please help me to honestly open my heart to my fellows regarding my transgressions so that I may move on from them. May we seek mutual intimacy and may others do the same in kind.

Glory to you Oh Lord, that you have provided me with a small, trusted group of companions who are open to hear my heart. As I unburden myself, the light of your truth can enter my soul and strengthen me in repentance. Please help me to always be willing to lend a listening ear to those who struggle, as I do, in their human condition and to be able to listen without judgment.

Amen

February 4

"In him we have redemption through his blood, the forgiveness of sins, in accordance with the riches of God's grace that he lavished on us." Ephesians 1:7

Dear Lord,

Thank you for your presence in my life. Thank you for how you continue to enter my life each day as I pour my heart out to you. You know my imperfections, my temptations and my doubts. You continue to hear the whisperings of my soul and strengthen me. Only your love is perfect and unfailing.

Please help me to offer grace and forgiveness to my fellows in kind. Help me not to hold onto resentment or to harbor negative thoughts about others. We are all fatally flawed human beings, made perfect only in your love. Please help me to reach for that each day instead of giving in to the calls of my lower instincts.

Amen

February 5

"You know what happened throughout the province of Judea, beginning in Galilee after the baptism that John preached." Acts 10:36

Dear Lord,

Open my heart today to receive the peace that the message of your love brings. Without the light of your love and guidance, I am lost. When left to my own devices, I am powerless against temptation. You purify my heart, Oh Lord, and provide the discernment required to navigate the pitfalls of life.

Please help me to always walk in your ways and not to waiver. Please help me to repay my debt to you by in turn proclaiming the glory of your unfailing love. I fall short each day, Oh Lord, yet the day begins anew each morning as I am fortified by your love and guidance. I keep my eye fixed on the prize of your unending love.

Amen

February 6

"He gives strength to the weary and increases the power of the weak." Isaiah 40:29

Dear Lord,

You are gracious and glorious. You hear my desperate cries for help and you fortify my soul. You guide me through days of darkness when I turn my face to your light. Alone, I am incapable of managing the difficulties of life. When filled up with your unending love, I feel as though I can move mountains.

Help me, Oh Lord, to be a beacon of light to the weak. May I help shine a light of your love on those who struggle in darkness. So many are hurting now, Oh Lord. So many are collapsing under the pressure of the loads they carry in this life. I too, had found myself at my breaking point. When I turn to you, however, you remove the trouble of my heart. Please help me always to remember that when I put you first, you carry me through the difficulties of my life.

Amen

February 7

"For our light and momentary troubles are achieving for us an eternal glory that far outweighs them all." 2 Corinthians 4:17

Dear Lord,

Please help me always to keep my sights on things above and not to get absorbed in the pain of this world. In a breath this life is gone, but the soul endures forever. In the end, I want to fly away. Please help me to live my life here in your heavenly presence. Please help me to be willing each day to surrender myself to your loving care.

My ego wants to hide and control, Oh Lord. I want to make myself Lord of my own life. Through the years I have learned that this does not work. It only leads to futility and unhappiness. It is only through following in the light of your ways that my heart is unburdened and I am able to walk in blessed assurance. My heart is aligned with you today, Oh Lord. I am filled with the light of your ways. You take my troubles away.

Glory and honor to you this day, Oh Lord.

Amen

February 8

"The mountains quake before him and the hills melt away."
Nahum 1:7

Dear Lord,

Only you know my true heart. You know my inner thought life; all my doubts and fears and my secret struggles. You know the troubles of my soul as I humble myself before you each day in prayer and petition. You are a good Lord. You hear me and you speak to me. You are my constant companion.

I trust that you will bless my life if I hold fast to your ways and remain willing to take direction. I hear you speak to me also through other believers as I open myself up to wise council when sin starts to fester in darkness. I keep nothing from you today, Lord. Take all of me, good and bad. Mold me and shape me to be closer to your likeness each day.

You are a good and glorious Lord.

Amen

February 9

"...He is our father in the sight of God, in whom he believed - the God who gives life to the dead and calls into being things that were not." Romans 4:17

Dear Glorious Lord,

I honor you today and give you thanks. You are like a parent to me. I come to you a broken and wounded child and you nourish me back to health. My soul was dead inside before being reawakened by your love. I am whole and sanctified by your love.

I am renewed each day as I pour out my soul to you and you hear my desperate cries for help. You take my sins and fortify me. You strengthen me each day as I build stamina to carry the burdens of life. Holy and honorable is your name. Please help me always to be willing to come to you as a child for you never disappoint and you always breathe life into my darkened soul.

Amen

February 10

"'You are my friends if you do what I command.'" John 15:14

Dear Lord,

I know I have a friend in you today. I am but a wretched sinner who gets lost daily in the ways of the world. When I draw near to you in reading your Word and praying, I learn. You show me how to respond to the challenges of life. You reveal yourself to me in my devotion. As I draw nearer to a community of believers who know the full range of my primal nature I receive godly council.

I am never alone, if I devote myself to you as your follower. Indeed, some days I am more resistant than others. You are always there, however, when I reach out to you. My life is not without its challenges, however, your love is unfailing. You honor me each day by showing up for me. Please help me to witness that to others who are suffering in the darkness.

Amen

February 11

"Pride goes before destruction, a haughty spirit before a fall." Proverbs 16:18

Dear Lord,

I need you daily by my side. I need your guidance and companionship. I also need to be able to pour my heart out to my fellows when I am struggling. My pride kicks in at times and I don't want to humble myself to ask for help. In the past, when I have approached my troubles in this fashion, I have allowed wounds to fester inside my soul and I eventually collapsed from stored pain.

Please help me always to remain willing to empty myself to you to receive guidance when I am unsure. When I am feeling hurt or lost, please help me to seek wise counsel. My life's work now is building a Godly fellowship about me to whom I can unveil my true heart.

Amen

February 12

"Preach the word; be prepared in season; correct, rebuke and encourage - with great patience and careful instruction."
2 Timothy 4:2

Dear Lord,

Please help me to stand firm in my beliefs and to gently assert my values with those that I invite into my life. Thank you for the community that is being built up around me; those who hear my struggles and those who are not afraid to speak your truth to me so that I may make course corrections to keep me on the narrow road.

Help me to always be willing to hear your gentle whispers. Please help me not to keep my motives a secret; as evil festers in the darkness. Light only lives in your true love as experienced through an honest community of believers. Please provide direction when I feel as though I have lost my way.

Amen

February 13

"For our struggle is not against flesh and blood, but against rulers, against the authorities, against the powers of this dark world and against the spiritual forces of evil in heavenly realms." Ephesians 6:12

Dear Lord,

The struggle is real. When I am weak, I constantly find myself compelled to allow forces of evil to be my master. Subtle messages invade my thoughts from TV, popular music and literature. I can create my own rules that can be derived solely from my earthly desires. I can give in to my secret desires and no one has to know.

Please help me always to make time, Oh Lord, to submit myself to you in prayer and to seek guidance in your Word. There are simple instructions that are clear. It I am still unconvinced, please help me to always be willing to seek godly counsel from others and to be honest in revealing my motives. Sometimes I am blinded to the deceptions of my own reasoning and I need a trusted third party to help me recognize that.

Amen

February 14

"An honest answer is like a kiss on the lips." Proverbs 24:26

Dear Lord,

I pour out my true heart to you. You know all of my successes and difficulties. You know my sins as well as my strengths. You hear my challenges and strengthen me. If I start scheming and hiding my motives from you, it blocks me from the light of the true Spriit.

Please help me always to keep my lines of communication with you open. Please help me to consistently lay my imperfections at your feet so that I may work each day to grow in your likeness. Help me not to revel in and glorify my primal nature today.

Thank you for loving me and for your endless grace. Each day I am made new as I empty myself and I allow you to fill me. Please work in and through me. Speak life through me to others who are also confronting their imperfections. We will never be like you, Oh Lord, but as we honestly open our hearts we will walk more and more in your way.

Amen

February 15

"And let us consider how we may spur one another on toward love and good deeds," Hebrews 10:24

Dear Lord,

Alone I am nothing, but through your love and the community around me I am enough. When I am lost on my path, I can turn to another believer for guidance and hope. I receive correction and gentle encouragement. Thank you for how you have blessed my life this day with my soul-tribe as it is building up around me.

My natural human condition is one of immaturity and selfishness. As I enter into partnership with others desiring a like connection with you, I make a movement toward a higher plane of existence. Those in my community encourage me when I am tempted to veer off course and give in to my primal nature. Please help me to always be willing to respond in kind to any of my fellows as they stumble along.

Amen

February 16

"Therefore, since we have these promises, dear friends, let us purify ourselves from everything that contaminates body and spirit, perfecting holiness out of reverence for God."
2 Corinthians 7:1

Dear Lord,

You help me purify my thoughts, words and actions when I lean in to you and ground myself in prayer and meditation on your Word. Glory and honor to you this day for how you bless me. When left to my own devices, my primal nature creeps in and overrides my best intentions.

Please help me always to be wary of the deceptiveness of my human tendencies. Please help me to constantly watch for selfishness and dishonesty in my motives. As I draw nearer to you each day the intricacies of my defects become more and more apparent. Please help me to learn to eventually be holy and blameless in your sight so that I may retreat to your comfort and care at the end of my days.

Amen

February 17

"'....Love your neighbor as yourself, there is no command greater than these.'" Mark 12:31

Dear Lord,

My peace and comfort in the joy of your love exists through community. When I am dwelling in my primal nature I experience fear, self-pity and an overall sense of lack. I start to feel as though I need to glean more than my fair share from the stream of life and that is hurtful to those about me. When I am walking in the light of your love, my cup is full and I can bring that to those I come into contact with.

Oh Lord, my God, please help me to always be mindful of how vital it is for me to fill myself with you each day. I need to pour out my worldly concerns and fill myself with your spirit. For when I do that I become a conduit of your love and I radiate harmony into the world about me. When I am stewing in my sin, I invite discord.

Oh Lord, most high, enter into our world at this time for we are in desperate need of learning how to follow your simple, yet very demanding commands.

Amen

February 18

"'and repentance for the forgiveness of sins will be preached in his name to all nations, beginning at Jerusalem.'" Luke 24:47

Dear Lord,

Thank you for providing us with your instructions for living. By nature, we humans are sinful beings. There is an inborn tendency for deception, fear and selfishness that causes all sorts of harm when not brought into the light of your love. Through an honest unveiling of my innermost thoughts both with you and with my fellows, I am blessed to be able to admit and turn away from my offenses. This is an ongoing process as new challenges present themselves each day.

Please help me to always remain willing to open my heart. I have my blind spots and I receive harsh criticisms regarding defects that I have hidden even from myself. Please help me to continue to add to my trusted circle of friends so as to continue to grow in your love and to invite others to step slowly out of the darkness.

Amen

February 19

"One who loves a pure heart and who speaks with grace will have the king for a friend." Proverbs 22:11

Dear Lord,

Please hear my heart today and help me to keep my sights fixed on things above. Please help me not to give in to my worldly urges to feed unbridled instincts. I want to attract only love into my life that is glorious and honorable in your sight. May I be deliberate in my thoughts, words and actions today.

There are many forces at work in the world that attempt to bend and pervert your Word. Only you, most high, speak the light of truth to my soul. Breathe into me and fill my cup when I empty myself to you. There are so many lost souls Oh Lord, please help me to be a guiding force and not to allow myself to veer off course to attend to petty disturbances.

It is only when my own light burns brightly that I can serve others.

Amen

February 20

"May God himself, the God of peace, sanctify you through and through. May your whole spirit, soul and body be kept blameless at the coming of our Lord Jesus Christ." 1 Thessalonians 5:23

Dear Lord,

I honor you on this day. You hear the outpouring of my human struggles and you wash my sins away. I am made new each morning as I seek direction in your Word. Listen to my heart, Oh Lord, and provide comfort and guidance.

You are available, Oh Lord, to all who earnestly seek. You are a light in the darkness of human confusion and suffering. I do not deserve to have you in my life, yet you continue to avail yourself to me each time I cry out. You take my sins and cleanse my soul. Oh gracious Lord, I am not worthy of you, yet you are my Lord.

Endless gratitude to you today.

Amen

February 21

"Not only so, but we also glory in our sufferings, because we know that suffering produces perseverance, perseverance, character and character, hope." Romans 5:3

Dear Lord,

I have known much suffering and I attract other wounded souls. Through your love, I find healing and I build strength for the road ahead. You test me daily. Please give me the stamina I need to make it to the finish line.

Maybe I thought as a young child that things would be different, more like a storybook or a Disney movie. I used to have resentments regarding all of the difficulties that I have been through in my life. Now I see that all of that was strength training so that I may go the distance. You provide guidance and support each day on my journey, when I ask for it.

Amen

February 22

"Be completely humble and gentle, be patient, bearing with one another in love." Ephesians 4:2

Dear Lord,

Please soften my heart and level my pride so that I may always be active in a faith community. Joining together in brotherly love to commune with other believers is a vital part of spiritual growth. I have you always in my heart, however. When isolated, deception creeps into my thoughts and darkness overtakes me.

Please help me always to remain willing to forgive mild offenses from others. I do know that I too will unknowingly offend. As our imperfections churn against each other, we become more polished and smooth, more like you in character. When alone, my defects grow and fester.

Thank you for the community that surrounds me today. Please help me to continue to foster its growth and development.

Amen

February 23

"And we know that in all things God works for the good of those that love him, who have been called according to his purpose." Romans 8:28

Dear God,

As I pray and meditate each day, your purpose for my life becomes clearer. I can lean into you and allow your words to guide my path. I can allow you to strengthen me in my walk. You bring the community I need closer to me to strengthen me in my trials.

I carry a heavy load, but you walk beside me. Teach me more and more each day how to walk in your ways. Your goodness is available to all and each one of us can step out of the darkness and be born into a purposeful, fulfilling life.

Amen

February 24

"I am your servant; give me discernment that I may understand your statutes," Psalm 119:125

Dear Lord,

I do not pretend to understand all of your commands. Throughout the journey of my life, I most certainly have not steered a straight and narrow course. You have rescued me, though, out of the furnace, because I have called on your holy name.

I still feel lost at times and overwhelmed by trouble. Your Word and your presence light my path and they are always available to me. You are kind and gracious, Oh Lord, because when I consult with you over difficult decisions, you do provide guidance. Please help me always to remain willing to do that and not to rely on my own ego and selfishness.

Amen

February 25

"'Do not judge, or you too will be judged.'" Matthew 7:1

Dear Lord,

You have blessed me and cleansed me of my sins. You have done this not only one time, but daily as I kneel before you and invite you in to provide strength in times of weakness. You are a good and gracious Lord and you avail yourself to all who earnestly seek.

Please help me to keep my heart and mind open in my evaluations and assessments of others. Please help me to be willing to grant them the same grace and tolerance that you have so lovingly given to me. Please grant me the wisdom to know when to disengage in sinful behavior and to learn how to love those involved from a distance so that I will not be pulled into sin.

You are a good and gracious Lord. Your love endures forever.

Amen

February 26

"But thanks be to God! He gives us victory through our Lord Jesus Christ." 1 Corinthians 15:57

Dear Lord,

Thank you for going to the cross for me. You take my shortcomings and provide me with victory over death. I am merely human. I fall short each day of your perfect image. Because of you, I can learn and grow in love and become nearer to your likeness.

Help me to always bear in mind the beauty of your grace. I don't have to be perfect today or any other day to be your servant. As a thank you to you for freeing me from the bondage of my sin, I commit myself to singing your praises to all those who may benefit from hearing the message of your unfailing love.

Amen

February 27

"Fools mock at making amends for sin, but goodwill is found among the upright." Proverbs 14:9

Dear Lord,

When I have a disturbance, your Word always points me in the right direction. I have learned over time that the mere grace of forgiveness is not always enough in regards to righting my wrongs. When my actions have selfishly harmed others, I often need to seek to personally right those wrongs.

Often, I want to sweep my wrongs under the carpet and blame the other party. Today my peace of mind depends upon my accountability. I cannot be a victim when I have done wrong. I need to seek to make things right, inasmuch as I am able to. When I earnestly seek to do your will, you provide guidance and direction in this area.

You are a good and gracious Lord and you avail yourself to all who seek.

Amen

February 28

"He makes me lie down in green pastures, he leads me beside still waters." Psalm 23:2

Dear Lord,

I lean into you, today and every day. I seek your will through daily prayer and meditation. You always provide guidance and direction when I move out of the driver's seat and let you take over. You provide abundantly for me and I am undeserving.

You help to quiet my busy mind and you give rest to my soul. This is available to all who earnestly seek. You have blessed me with an amazing life. I walk in nature, in the wonder of your creation, and you guide and direct my path. You reassure me each day by showing me the beauty of your heavenly kingdom here on earth.

Glory and honor to you this day, Oh Lord.

February 29

"A gentle answer turns away wrath, but a harsh word stirs up anger." Proverbs 15:1

Dear Lord,

Help me to be firm with my boundaries but not to be harsh or insensitive with the individuals. I desire to gently instruct and not to demean or blame. I desire to be compassionate of others and to allow them to step into the light of your presence through me. Yet, at the same time, help me not to allow myself to be pulled into the darkness.

Rather than arguing with those who are ensnared in sinful behavior, please help me to first commune with others who walk in the light. Help me send clear, concise messages that, in order to be in my company, the student must be willing to align in higher ways. It is a fault of mine, Oh Lord, that I am too tolerant of sin and I occasionally become ensnared by association.

Through your grace, I can step back into the light, but this causes me unnecessary disturbances. Thank you, Oh Lord, for my community who rebuke me in love when I am walking in the danger zone.

Amen

March 1

"Humility is the fear of the Lord; Its wages are riches and honor and life." Proverbs 22:4

Dear Lord,

I am abundantly blessed today, thank you for looking after me when I keep my head down and busy myself in following your your commands. All I have comes from you. You are the Lord of my life. You guide my thoughts, words and actions when I remind myself to earnestly seek.

When I exalt myself and try to rely on my own understanding, you continue to love me. You provide gentle corrections and allow me the opportunity to get back on track. Your love is unfailing when I am in abeyance of your principles. I am not perfect, I fall short of your glory each day, but you continue to love and bless me as long as I surrender my heart and mind to you.

Amen

March 2

"Do you not know that in a race all runners run, but only one gets the prize? Run in such a way as to get the prize."
1 Corinthians 9:24-25

Dear Lord,

Please help me to keep my eyes focused on the prize at all times. There are a lot of distractions that come up and I am tempted to let them have my attention. Please help me to keep my head down and to focus my feet on moving in the right direction, when I am feeling stuck.

As I continue to draw nearer to you, I come closer to your consciousness. I begin to understand more of your plan for my life and I feel more directed. You fortify and strengthen me each day to resist what you know I need to. When I am walking in the light and allowing you to guide my way, I invite delight and positivity into my life and my relationships.

Amen

March 3

"Therefore, I urge you, brothers and sisters, in view of God's mercy, to offer your bodies as a living sacrifice, holy and pleasing to God - this is your prue and proper worship." Romans 12:1

Dear Lord,

I am endlessly grateful to you for the grace you show me. I am a new creation in your love each day as I surrender myself wholly to you. Guide me and direct me to always seek you first and to let everything else fall into place around that primary relationship.

Please Lord, rid me of the bondage of self and bring the right people into my path to whom I may witness the miracle of your presence. You have rescued me from the prison of my sin. You invite me in my brokenness into the glory of your kingdom. Your kingdom is open to all who seek to walk in your ways.

Glory to you this day, Oh Lord.

March 4

"Finally, brothers and sisters, whatever is right, whatever is pure, whatever is lovely, whatever is admirable - if anything is excellent or praiseworthy - think about such things." Philippians 4:8

Dear Lord,

I have an active thought life. Many things run through my mind. I often feel as though my mind is a runaway train. Please help me, dear Lord, to always be willing to carve out my meditation time talking to you, listening to you and reading the Word.

When I invite you into my mind, I have more ammunition to combat the negativity in my mind. I have good and evil sides to my thought-life. When I feed the goodness, it grows. When I feed the darkness, the helplessness, fear and depression grow. You speak to me of hope and of light. Please help me always be willing to allow you to redirect me when I get pulled into worldly distractions.

Your ways are goodness, purity and love.

Amen

March 5

"The grace of our Lord was poured out on me abundantly, along with faith and love that are in Christ Jesus." 1 Timothy 1:14

Dear Lord,

Thank you for pouring yourself out into me so graciously. I do not deserve your love and honor, Oh Lord. You have rescued me from a life of sin. You paid a debt for me and I am eternally grateful. May I live my life as a living sacrifice to you.

You bring me into a community with all who belong to me in your love. I am free today from bondage because of your love and care. I have a faithful knowledge of you that dwells within me for others to see. You are the goodness and the light that I seek.

Amen

March 6

"A generous person will prosper; whoever refreshes others will be refreshed." Proverbs 11:25

Dear Lord,

It is a giving season. Please bring the right people into my life that I am able to help according to my gifts. When I keep my heart open and make my daily connection with you, you bring me into contact with those that I may contribute to according to my blessings.

When I seek to find how I can help others and step out of my selfish tendencies, you bless my life. When I give, I receive more of your abundance. I have more than I deserve, due to the fact that I seek to give generously to others and to those who do the work of your kingdom.

Your Word provides guidance and direction in my life, Oh Lord.

Amen

March 7

"Do not let any unwholesome talk come out of your mouths, but only what is helpful for building others up according to their needs, that it may benefit those who listen." Ephesians 4:29

Dear Lord,

Please help me to be careful with my speech and to use wholesome language that is not harsh or critical. I desire to be inclusive with my language, never exclusive, oh Lord, in providing corrections to others. Please help me always to do so out of love, not out of scorn or retaliation.

As you have loved me through my trials and shortcomings, please help me to do the same for others. Please help me to always speak in kindness and love so that I may draw others closer to you through my words. You have delivered me from a prison of torment. For that I rejoice and I invite others into the spirit of your lovingkindness through a true experience of Christian love.

Amen

March 8

"But if you harbor bitter envy or selfish ambition in your hearts, do not boast about it or deny the truth." James 3:14

Dear Lord,

Please help me to be willing to let go of any selfish or ego-driven thoughts that may cross my mind. I am human, thus rather than admit my shortcomings, I often prefer to blame and rationalize. Please help me to be willing today to take the high road. I want to grow in your likeness.

When I am willing to admit to the folly of my ways, I take the path of spiritual growth. In doing so, I invite into my life other like-minded souls. As I walk in this community, I come closer to your grace. In that place I am strengthened and fortified so that I may instruct others who are also struggling in bondage.

There is a way through to the light of your truth, Oh Lord.

Amen

March 9

"But I am afraid that just as Eve was deceived by the serpent's cunning, your minds may somehow be led astray from your sincere and pure devotion to Christ."
2 Corinthians 11:3

Dear Lord,

Help me please, not to follow the train of thought that enters my mind when I am tempted to go against your ways. I desire to devote my life wholly and fully to you so that I may reap my rewards and rest in eternal peace. Today I suffer from the bondage of my human condition.

I turn my sights to you and on what is pure in your sight. Some days I walk convicted in my path, other days I waiver. I am gifted in that, I have a close community around me who strengthen and fortify me when I am weak. Let us all do that for each other, Oh Lord. Let us listen with discerning guidance when others seek council so that we may receive it in return.

Amen

March 10

"Praise be to God the Father of our Lord Jesus Christ, who has blessed us in heavenly realms with every spiritual blessing in Christ." Ephesians 1:3

Dear Lord,

You are a righteous and glorious Lord. I try in the best manner I can to study your Word and to follow in your ways and I am abundantly blessed. All that I have and all I am comes from you. I feel alive with the spirit and I know that you have not forgotten me.

I feel close to you today and I take joy in your presence. Some days I am close to you and some days I am further away. You are unwavering. You never move, but I pull myself further away by my own behavior. When I walk in the light you honor me, when I stumble, that disconnects me. There has always been a way back, Lord.

Your love is unfailing, Lord.

March 11

"The Lord will rescue me from every evil attack and will bring me safely to his heavenly kingdom." 2 Timothy 4:18

Dear Lord,

I know that you will deliver comfort and care, provided I stay the course and follow your commands. Trials come occasionally, the load can get heavy, but I continue to study your Word and connect with you each day. I pray and meditate and the path becomes clearer.

Some days are dark and confusing. There are other days where I rest in assurance, aware of your comfort and care. On the difficult days, I lean in harder to you. I seek more and more to hear you speak to me. There is an easy path out of my suffering, and then there is the godly course which is always more work. When I diligently follow in your ways, I have the safety of your wisdom.

Amen

March 12

"'Who can hide in secret places so that I cannot see them?' declares the Lord. 'Do I not fill heaven and earth?' declares the Lord" Jeremiah 23:24

Dear Lord,

Please help me always to be willing to examine my thoughts and motives. Sometimes I am tempted to do things that I don't want anyone to know about. I know that you know my true heart and my struggles.

It is important, however, for me to bring my transgressions to you directly. I need to own them and lay them at your feet so that you may remove them and cleanse me. You are so praiseworthy, Oh Lord, that you offer your grace to me. I am not worthy of your forgiveness and yet you offer it to me so freely anyway.

Amen

March 13

"Trust in the Lord with all your heart and lean not on your own understanding" Proverbs 3:5

Dear Lord,

I surrender to you today. I trust that you will bring goodness, light and joy into my life provided that I stay close to you. I am but a humble human being. Sometimes I drive myself crazy trying to orchestrate a plan. I know that this is not my place, Lord. Only you know how the pieces will come together.

My place is not to control the outcome or write the script. My place is to honestly seek you each day through devoted prayer and meditation. In doing so, you reveal messages and signs. You guide my way and light my path. As long as I do not veer off course I know that I will receive the promises of your kingdom.

Amen

March 14

"'Ask and it will be given to you; seek and you will find; knock and the door will be opened to you.'" Matthew 7:7

Dear Lord,

You are a gracious Lord. As I pray and seek you boldly each day, you manifest more and more in my life. When I petition you in an appropriate manner, and follow with right action, you carry me through my struggles. As I study your Word each day and open myself to receive you, you reveal yourself.

Your divine light is available to all who choose to take this path. As you have embraced me in my wretchedness, you avail yourself to anyone. You have blessed me tenfold since I began on my journey. You have proven yourself to me time and time again. You open your arms to me when I am hurting to provide comfort.

Please help more people to know you as I do, as a trusted companion and friend.

March 15

"For through the Spirit we eagerly await by faith the righteousness for which we hope." Galatians 5:5

Dear Lord,

I seek to follow you today and not be led astray by worldly concerns. Your Word is clear that if I live in abeyance of your commands I will unite victoriously with you in your kingdom. I have faith today in the promise of your Word and I seek to follow in your ways.

My intentions are good at the beginning of each day, but as the days wear on, I often veer off course. I try to do too much, be too much. I want too much. At this moment, Lord, your love is enough. You provide for and fill my heart with all the abundance that I need to get through the day. This is provided through unwavering faith.

Please help me to stay grounded and focused on your kingdom, oh Lord. Let me set my sights on things above.

Amen

March 16

"I will consider all your works and meditate on all your mighty deeds." Psalm 77:12

Dear Lord,

Each day I look for guidance in your Word. Each day I pray and seek you. In return you strengthen me and give me what I need to get through the day. Some days are more difficult than others. Sometimes I make them so.

I can always return to you at any point during the day the day if I get off track. The more I meditate on your Word the more it becomes ingrained in me. Your Word is the armor that strengthens me against the difficulties of the world. When I come to you in the morning, I strip myself bare and pour out my heart. Each day you fill me up.

You are available to all who earnestly seek, Oh Lord.

Amen

March 17

"'Therefore everyone who hears these words of mine and puts them into practice is like a wise man who built his house on the rock." Matthew 7:24

Dear Lord,

I am but a humble human. I do not follow your commands perfectly. However, each day I diligently seek to follow your will. You have abundantly blessed my life as a result and I overflow with gratitude. All of my blessings are grounded in you and I maintain awareness of that.

I know that if I lose sight of the journey that I travel toward your blessed kingdom, all will be lost for me. My empire of blessings increases daily through faith. Your love and presence in my life are the foundations from which all blessings flow.

Help me to hold firm and not to be pulled off course, dear Lord.

Amen

March 18

"...'Truly I tell you, unless you change and become like little children, you will never enter the kingdom of heaven.'"
Matthew 18:3

Dear Lord,

When it comes to learning to walk in your ways, please help me to be willing to completely surrender my ego. Each day new challenges arise and I cannot lean on my understanding. I need to empty myself to you each day. I need to humble myself like a child and to allow you to fill me and strengthen me for the day ahead.

The days when I feel confident and as though I know what I am doing are the days that I need to watch out. I need to constantly give my own power over to you so that you may guide and direct me. It is only in doing so that I equip myself to walk steadfast, on this road to your kingdom.

Amen

March 19

"'Blessed are those who hunger and thirst for righteousness, for they will be filled.'" Matthew 5:6

Dear Lord,

I do not follow perfectly in your ways. I am humble and I stumble sometimes. I do diligently seek you each morning in devotion and pray that your path will be revealed to me. Sometimes the message is unclear. In those times I find it best to pause a day, a week, a month, possibly longer, without taking an action.

In the past, I have found that decisions made in haste have caused me to drift off course. I do find that as I make a priority out of seeking right action, I am rewarded. The reward is not always matching my desire, but it always fills a need. Please help me to remember your strength and guidance prior to responding in spontaneous action. For when I seek you first, my cup is abundantly filled.

Amen

March 20

"Love is patient, love is kind. It does not envy, it does not boast, it is not proud." 1 Corinthians 13:4

Dear Lord,

As I go through life, I realize that there are many sentiments that easily get confused with love. If I have an inclination to rush into a closeness with someone, that is not love. If I have to talk myself up to or prove myself, that is not love. If I feel that I have to take from another to get what I want, that is not love.

True love waits for the right moment. It builds up and edifies. It is unconditional and I do not have to sell myself short to receive it. When I put you first, Lord, I invite others into that love. That is the type of pure, unwavering love that I want to radiate into my life today.

You are a perfect father, Lord. May I do my best to imitate you in my relationships today.

Amen

March 21

"Though the Lord is exalted, he looks kindly on the lowly; though lofty, he sees them from afar." Psalm 138:6

Dear Lord,

Help me to always remain willing to humble myself to you. When I look up to you each day, you empower me in my smallness and make me capable. When I am coming from a place that is ego driven, I am setting myself up for a fall. Regardless of my achievements, I need to always remember you are above me.

I pour myself out to you today, Lord. I lay my faults at your feet. You know my heart. Please remove all that blocks me from participating in true communion with you. As I do this each day, your power flows in and builds me up for the day ahead, regardless of how challenging it is.

I honor your ways, oh Lord, although I do not always understand them.

Amen

March 22

"Then you will know the truth and the truth will set you free." John 8:32

Dear Lord,

Please reveal your truth to me more and more each day as I continually seek your guidance. I have many trials and struggles over which I am conflicted. Today, instead of acting on impulse, I will wait until your voice is clear. If I am wanting something and I am not receiving clarity on it directly from you, I will pause and wait.

When I don't know your will or when I am torn in regards to how to proceed, I will wait until you reveal yourself. When my will takes over and I try to force things that I want, things start to go wrong. I need to pay attention to my motives and to how your truth manifests itself in my life.

I am open to hearing you today, Oh Lord. I will heed your call, even if I don't like the message.

Amen

March 23

"The plans of the diligent lead to profit as surely as haste leads to poverty." Proverbs 21:5

Dear Lord,

I seek your will today, Oh Lord, and I seek to walk in your ways. When I diligently follow in your ways, your blessings abound. I am a mere human, Lord. I stumble and falter, but I get up and realign myself with your commands. I am blessed abundantly today and, despite my many trials, I have community support.

I was a lowly, wretched soul and I was rescued by your goodness and grace. I have taken your yoke upon me and you have exceeded my hopes and dreams in how you have blessed my life. I live simply and have much to share when I encounter other seekers along the way.

Amen

March 24

"not looking to your own interests but each of you to the interests of others. In your relationships with one another have the same mindset as Christ Jesus." Philippians 2:4-5

Dear Lord,

Please help me to always remember to invite pure Christian love into my relationships. There are times as I go through my day where I may be tempted to react in fear or from a place of selfish inconsideration. Please help me to acknowledge the godly light in each soul and to be willing to pause before reacting.

For you, Oh Lord, have taken all of me, including my imperfections. Please help me to approach others in this fashion as well. At the same time, I need to watch out not to be pulled into sin by another.

Please give me discernment in my relations and help me to tread lightly today.

Amen

March 25

"and once made perfect, he became the source of eternal salvation for all who obey him." Hebrews 5:9

Dear God,

I have invited you into my soul and I will do my best to follow your commands. May I always be willing to follow you and your ways. There are times when I am tempted to go astray and I am unclear of how to proceed. Wise counsel can be helpful, but ultimately you are my guiding force.

Only you know my true heart, Lord. Only you know the right path for me to take to reach my destination. You reveal yourself more and more each day and I know that I have good things ahead of me. You are a holy and righteous Lord. You provide deliverance from my suffering.

Glory and honor to you today, Oh Lord.

Amen

March 26

"Recalling your tears, I long to see you so that I may be filled with joy." 2 Timothy 1:4

Dear Lord,

Pain is inevitable in this life. There are sickness disease, death, war, murder and many other horrible things. It can wear on us; break us down slowly over time. Your Word is clear, however, that we do not belong to this world. Our deliverance will come in the end if we keep our sights on things above.

Of course we are human, Lord. Of course we stumble at times or falter. But you provide your strength as we study your Word, and deeply surrender ourselves to you in prayer. There are times when our paths are unclear. We may ask 100 different people how to proceed and we may get 100 different answers. Only you can give us the right answers, Lord. You always reveal yourself in time.

Amen

March 27

"But I trust in your unfailing love; my heart rejoices in your salvation." Psalm 13:5

Dear Lord,

I draw near to you today. I feel your closeness and your presence. You reveal yourself to me in quiet times of devotion and prayer. You reassure me that my salvation is pure and that the slate has been wiped clean. You give me blessed assurance that I will be delivered from my trials.

You have secured a place for me, unworthy as I may be. I feel your divine light and love in my soul. I open my heart today to hear your truth and I know that you have good things in store for me. I take refuge in your love. This soul sanctuary is available to all.

Amen

March 28

"If it is possible, as far as it depends on you, live at peace with everyone." Romans 12:18

Dear Lord,

Please help me to put my ego aside as I interact with others. Help me to show humility and understanding in regards to differences of opinion. Help me to be a peacemaker in times of conflict. At the same time, however, please help me to be able to make my voice heard.

I have value in your kingdom today, dear Lord, as I shine your loving light on all I come into contact with. As I learn to deliver peace in my surroundings, I build community. You have blessed me with an amazing circle of friends and you bring the same peace and acceptance to my life.

You are a good and gracious Lord.

Amen

March 29

"Therefore, as God's chosen people, holy and dearly loved, clothe yourselves with compassion, kindness, humility, gentleness and patience." Colossians 3:12

Dear Lord,

I humble my heart to you today so that I may hear your voice as it whispers to my soul. I tune into your people, your blessed community, so that my behaviors and lifestyle choices may be holy and righteous in your site. I approach my decisions and interactions with tenderness and gentleness.

When I am troubled or morally conflicted, I pause and patiently wait for you to speak to me. I do not take the next action until I am clear about your divine guidance. Please help me to be ever able to nurture the maturity needed to be careful, kind, directed, and patient in all decisions. I will wait for your appointed time. I know you have good things in store for me.

Amen

March 30

"Trust in the Lord forever, for the Lord, the Lord himself, is the Rock eternal." Isaiah 26:4

Dear Lord,

I trust you today. I make you the Lord of my life. I serve you and you provide for me each day, bountifully. Please help me to remember that I do not have to carry the heavy weight of my burdens alone when I am feeling weighed down and overwhelmed. I am trusting you and your promise of delivering me from my suffering.

I have been able to carry a heavy load throughout my life as a result of your grace and kindness. When I am in doubt of your ability to hold me up through my trials, you have a proven track record of always carrying me when I allow it.

You are a good and gracious Lord who avails himself to all who earnestly seek.

Amen

March 31

"Whoever dwells in the shelter of the Most High will rest in the shadow of the Almighty." Psalm 91:1

Dear Lord,

Today you carve out a space for me in your loving arms. In times of trouble you comfort me with the shelter of your love. You carry me through with the strength of your divine presence. You provide community and safety when I am under attack.

Please help me to never allow anything or anyone to sever the bond I have with you. Without you I am lost and I become easy prey for the demons of this world. With you I have peace and comfort.

You are a good and gracious Lord, Oh God. You avail yourself to all who seek.

Amen

April 1

"But thanks to God! He gives us victory through our Lord Jesus Christ." 1 Corinthians 15:57

Dear Lord,

You walk with me through troubled times. When I plead with you, you guide my thoughts, words and actions. You speak through me into the hearts of others. As I struggle you give me victory over my obstacles. When I put you first, when I fix my sights on you, you give me victory over all obstacles.

As you fill me up each day, I quietly gain power to combat destructive forces. Your goodness lives within me, provided I invite it in each day. Please help me to always be mindful of your delicate gift and how quickly the fall from grace can occur if I fail to maintain my daily connection with you.

Amen

April 2

"Here is a trustworthy saying that deserves full acceptance: Christ Jesus came into the world to save sinners – of whom I am the worst." 1 Timothy 1:15

Dear Lord,

You have saved me despite my wretchedness. You are a holy and righteous Lord. I do not deserve you, yet you come to me each day and you offer your grace and mercy. I make you Lord of my life today and you guide me and direct me.

Please help me to offer that grace to all with whom I come into contact. Please help me not to judge and place blame. Please help me to approach all with kindness and tolerance knowing that all are facing some kind of battle.

Amen

April 3

"My brothers and sisters, take note of this: Everyone should be quick to listen, slow to speak and slow to become angry"
James 1:19

Dear Lord,

Please guide my thoughts, words and actions today as I approach difficult conversations. Please help me to be kind and merciful, yet at the same time, not to allow impurity into my life. As I minister to others, I often find it difficult to walk the line between tolerance and spiritual invasion.

When I experience an attack, often my first instinct comes from fear. When I am in the space of fear, I cannot be fully of service. I am acting from a place of ego and selfishness. When I respond in love, I am protected and respected. If I feel wounded or threatened from attack, please help me to summon the spirit and breathe life into that space in my soul so that you may speak through me.

Amen

April 4

"What good is it, my brothers and sisters, if someone claims to have faith but has no deeds? Can such faith save them?"
James 2:14

Dear Lord,

You show yourself in my life each day as I seek you. As I draw nearer to you, your plan for my life becomes clearer and clearer. I no longer doubt you and I know that you have good things in store for me provided I stay close to you and listen to how you reveal yourself to me each day.

This work is a living testimony of how I experience you as you manifest yourself in my life. Faithful deeds appear in a variety of ways. You call your servants to action according to their abilities. Each follower has unique gifts to bring to the table. As we grow in relationship to you the plan of action becomes clearer.

Glory to you today Oh Lord.

April 5

"Above all else guard your heart, for everything you do flows from it." Proverbs 4:23

Dear Lord,

I seek to diligently fix my sights on you today. I guard my heart and seek to align myself with others who are of a similar mindset. Please help me to be convicted and principled in relations. There is a tendency to be reckless in matters of the heart. This has no place in your kingdom nor in my life.

I invite you into my heart, mind, body and soul. I request your guidance, care and protection. Your love is steady and you provide wisdom when I fix my sights on you. When my head is clear, my intuition regarding friendship and companionship is trustworthy.

You are honorable, Oh Lord. You are my primary intimate relationship.

Amen

April 6

"Endure hardship as discipline; God is treating you as his children. For what children are not disciplined by their father?" Hebrews 12:7

Dear Lord,

When I feel your hand on me in discipline, it is uncomfortable. It redirects me out of the comforts of my sinful behaviors and urges me back onto the narrow path toward your kingdom. Sometimes I go into a dark place. I think that this discomfort is a punishment. I think it means that you do not love me.

Quite the contrary, Oh Lord. I know now that your discipline is out of love. You want to train me to walk in your ways. You want to draw me closer to you each day like a loving father. You clearly redirect me when I get off course, as I have a tendency to do.

You bless my life with your words, Oh Lord.

Amen

April 7

"The eyes of all look to you, and you give them food at the proper time." Proverbs 145:15

Dear Lord,

There are many elements to a full and happy life. When I am living in my humanness I can drift into worry and anxiety as I am lacking and I need to shift my focus. When I fix my sights on you I invite goodness and abundance.

I put my trust in you today, Oh Lord, and you provide. You hear my secret prayers and you provide for my needs. You are a good father. You demand work from me. You do not hand me life on a silver platter. When I do the footwork, Oh Lord, you always deliver your comfort and care in miraculous ways.

I listen closely and you direct my actions.

Amen

April 8

"So do not fear, for I am with you; do not be dismayed, for I am your God. I will strengthen you and help you; I will uphold you with my righteous right hand." Isaiah 41:10

Dear Lord,

There are many things in this life that trigger my fear instinct. So many things are uncertain and it is easy to get lost and confused. As long as I put you first and diligently seek you each day you strengthen me and help me. You guide me along my journey and light my way.

Please help me to remember that you are my constant companion. I do not have to trudge this road alone. You are always available to me. With you by my side I have nothing to fear. I want to always put you first and to follow in your ways.

Amen

April 9

"In the same way, count yourselves dead to sin, but alive to God in Christ Jesus." Romans 6:11

Dear Lord,

You breathe new life into my previously dead soul. You fill my spirit and bless me bountifully each day. Please help me to be a ray of light to all who live in the darkness. There is hope for all.

No sin is too grave to be lifted away. No life is too insignificant. It is never too late to be made new in Christ Jesus. I repent and renew each morning as I empty myself and fill my cup with your love.

You are a great and glorious Lord. You guide my path and draw goodness near to me when I follow in your ways.

Amen

April 10

"I can do all this through him who gives me strength."
Philippians 4:13

Dear Lord,

Sometimes my weight in this world is heavy. Sometimes the load I carry seems cumbersome. I give my will and my life completely over to you each day. You fill me up and you carry me when I earnestly breathe out self-will and ego-dependance.

I need you more and more each day, dear Lord as the troubles of this life do not stop. There is no escape from the pain and brokenness of this world. The only comfort is in you, Oh Lord and in the amazing community of believers that you bring to me to lift me up. I am strengthened daily through prayer, meditation and genuine fellowship.

You provide for my needs, Oh Lord. Your love is unfailing.

Amen

April 11

"'Therefore do not worry about tomorrow, for tomorrow will worry about itself. Each day has enough trouble of its own.'" Matthew 6:14

Dear Lord,

Sometimes I have a busy mind. I try to predict the future or think about everything that could go wrong. I try to orchestrate and plan. I forget that all I need to do each day in every moment is seek your will and perform your work well.

All each one of us has is now. Whatever happened yesterday is history. This present moment has everything we need to secure our place in your kingdom. Boldly confronting the troubles of today insures a smoother tomorrow both here and in the hereafter.

Amen

April 12

"Let us examine our ways and test them, and let us return to the Lord." Lamentations 3:40

Dear Lord,

I lay my troubles at your feet today. I pour myself out to you and I ask you to fill me up. Please direct my thoughts, words and actions. Please help my ego to take a back seat to your guidance and direction.

Primal nature is something that never leaves us. Each day I need to evaluate my thoughts and behavior and realign them with your ways. I do have moments where I get out of alignment and forget to check myself.

Your grace is unending and you continue to hear my heart. You step into my darkened soul and light my day. Forgive me for the transgressions of yesterday.

Amen

April 13

"But you, Lord, are a shield around me, my glory, the One who lifts my head high." Psalm 3:3

Dear Lord,

I honor you today. You protect me from my enemies and provide me with strength and shelter. My trials are many, but you provide deliverance from suffering. In the eye of the storm I sit, with life whirling around me.

You are my comfort, Oh Lord; my shield. So long as I seek to walk in your ways you carry me through this life. The light of your love is available to all.

You are my close confidant, my treasured friend.

Amen

April 14

"Get rid of all bitterness, rage and anger, brawling and slander, along with every form of malice." Ephesians 4:31

Dear Lord,

I have fully opened my heart up to you. I accept your light and love into my soul today. I have no room in my life for hate. When anger comes, I let it wash over me like a wave. I do not hold onto it.

Although I may not be attracted to everyone I meet, Oh Lord, please help me to lay down all animosity. There are different paths for different people. Judgment can be a tool of evil and I need to lay that down a lot of times as well.

Please Lord, always guide my thoughts, words and actions so that I am coming from a place of kindness.

Amen

April 15

"He has made everything beautiful in its time. He has also set eternity in the human heart; yet no one can fathom what God has done from beginning to end." Ecclesiastes 3:11

Dear Lord,

The beauty of your kingdom defies explanation. Here on earth, we only touch the surface of your vast capabilities. I am blessed to be a part of your divine creation. Help me never to lose sight of your divine spirit as it lives in me.

As I nurture that spirit each day, my light shines brighter and I draw like-minded souls toward me. This loving communion generates more divinity. You have taken me, the wretched soul that I was and enveloped me in the beauty of your kingdom.

I am in awe of you today and in the glory of your good works.

Amen

April 16

"for I know that through your prayers and God's provision of the Spirit of Jesus Christ what has happened to me will turn out for my deliverance." Philippians 1:19

Dear Lord,

I find your presence in the community of other believers. You enter my soul as I open myself up to the spirit and to other believers. You fill up the dark space in my soul with light and you carry me through many trials.

When I can't pray for myself, Lord, others do it for me. I have a fellowship that supports me and we lift each other up. We trudge this road together and keep each other on track. In our shared brokenness we are made complete through your love.

You deliver us from suffering and provide vital, loving communion with one another. Your love is unfailing.

Amen

April 17

"When anxiety was great within me, your consolation brought me joy." Psalm 94:19

Dear Lord,

I pour out my heart to you today. I empty myself of all confusion and uncertainty. I give you all of my worries and fears. You take them and give me the joy of your indwelling spirit.

Although I have many desires, you have provided for all of my needs. As long as I put you first and remain in humble servitude, the light of your love fills me. Aging, sickness and loss, all of these bring hardship. As long as I stay deeply rooted in faith, the joy of the Lord belongs to me.

May I always be a light to those in doubt and fear.

Amen

April 18

"Frustration is better than laughter, because a sad face is good for the heart. The heart of the wise is in the house of mourning, but the heart of the fool is in the house of pleasure." Ecclesiastes 7:3-4

Dear Lord,

As I follow your call, Oh Lord, I look around me at times and feel as though I'm missing out. I experience the pain of the world deeply. I grieve. I mourn. I cry.

I look around me and I see others enthralled in pleasurable distraction. As I dive deeply into your Word, I am reminded that I need to experience this life fully in order to transition to the next. I cannot numb the pain. I need to find my truth and your divinity in the brokenness of this life. Your love envelops me and carries me through.

We all have a unique life experience but no one is alone. Oh Lord, you are my faithful companion.

Amen

April 19

"Crowds gathered also from the towns around Jerusalem, bringing their sick and those tormented by impure spirits, and all of them were healed." Acts 5:16

Dear Lord,

We live in a world with much sickness, affliction and pain. Your spirit has entered me and cleared my afflicted mind. To you I give all glory and honor for this healing. You have brought into my life the right community and treatment that was needed to rid me of the affliction. I continue to maintain my humility and my daily need for your help and guidance.

Although you do not heal everyone in their earthly form, my gratitude abounds in servitude. I look after the unhealthy as an expression of your blessing in my life. May I carry your light to the afflicted and shine your divine light.

All glory and honor is yours today, Oh Lord.

Amen

April 20

"That is why, for Christ's sake, I delight in weaknesses, in insults, in hardships, in persecutions, in difficulties. For when I am weak, I am strong." 2 Corinthians 12:10

Dear Lord,

Although the joy of your love is abundant, the pain and suffering of this life is unavoidable. As I turn to you each day, you strengthen me and carry me through my difficulties. As I continue to diligently allow you into my heart I become stronger, more able to endure and persevere.

In doing so, I develop character which I use to support others. Your light shines in me as a beacon of hope to those in darkness. My community also provides me with hope in my suffering.

Today I invite the spirit in. Your hope reigns eternal.

Amen

April 21

"For his anger lasts only a moment, but his favor lasts a lifetime; weeping may stay for the night, but rejoicing comes in the morning." Psalm 30:5

Dear Lord,

From time to time, my struggles and fears run through my mind. I think about my flaws and how I have failed you and I become restless. I breathe you in and exhale the struggles of each day.

I wake up rested and in your loving presence. I praise you as you allow me a fresh start each day. Each day is full of its own challenges and, each day I miss the mark of walking in your perfect image. I learn, I grow in my understanding and I become more human.

You embrace me in your grace and for this I come to you in loving gratitude.

Amen

April 22

"But I have calmed and quieted myself, I am like a weaned child with its mother; like a weaned child I am content." Psalm 131:2

Dear Lord,

My soul finds comfort in you today. You bring me into the exact right interdependent relation with the community about me. I do not cling too tightly to any one person. I receive love from you but also through my various relationships.

Please help me to be able to transmit light and love to those about me. Your Word breathes insight as well as prayer and careful study. In this way I can better apply your instructions to my daily life. I sin each day, and miss the mark.

I pray, dear Lord, that I can grow closer to your perfect ideal each day.

Amen

April 23

"'For where two or three are gathered in my name, there I am with them.'" Matthew 18:20

Dear Lord,

It is nice to have a faith community to be involved with. In my case, at this time, it is not possible for me to go to a building to worship. You bless me today as you bring into my life a healthy community of like-minded folk. When I open my heart in genuine communion, you fill me with your guidance and direction.

Today I am broken open and restored to wholeness through the fellowship about me. You meet me where I am and you lift me up. Your love is available to all. No one needs to manage the burdens of this life alone.

I invite all who suffer alone into loving communion here.

Amen

April 24

"As a father has compassion on his children, so the Lord has compassion on those who fear him" Psalm 103:13

Dear Lord,

Not one of us is perfect. Each evening as I analyze the actions, thoughts and words of the day, I fall short. Your grace covers me as I strive to do better. When I am in sin, I separate myself from you. I don't like living in the darkness. I want your light to shine upon me.

I am human and flawed, yet you continue to love me anew each day. You take all of my fears and when I honestly seek, you provide guidance. Your loving community embraces me in my brokenness. You love me not in spite of my fears, but because of them.

Amen

April 25

"So it is with you, since you are eager for gifts of the Spirit, try to excel in those that build up the church." 1 Corinthians 14:12

Dear Lord,

I thirst for spiritual nourishment. I draw nearer to you each day in devotion to improve my character and walk more in your likeness. It is most important for me to walk in humility so that I may not pollute your message with vain conceit.

Egos and power struggles break down the fabric of your holy community. They do not fortify or strengthen anything. You draw me nearer each day with your tenderness and kindness. As you fill me up, I attract others to me to commune in that presence.

The church is not the building. The church is your holy community of loving believers.

Amen

April 26

"I call out to the Lord, and he answers me from his holy mountain." Psalm 3:4

Dear Lord,

I have laid many petitions at your feet. You take my troubles and you provide comfort and care. I cry for you in silence and you provide guidance and solace. Each day your plan for my life more clearly unfolds in front of me.

You are gracious to enter my life in this way. You assure me in my doubt. You are my best friend and closest confidant. Around that relationship springs up genuine, like-minded fellowship. It is a fellowship that graces me lovingly each day with unfailing love.

My trials are many, but you fortify me with your strength. For this I am eternally grateful.

Amen

April 27

"The Lord is close to the brokenhearted and saves those who are crushed in spirit." Psalm 34:18

Dear Lord,

The trials of the world can wear me down. I am broken and downtrodden. Your Word lifts me up with hope. I invite you into my spirit today to provide warmth and comfort. Some days it is easier to let go of worldly cares than others. Some days I cling too tightly to earthly concerns.

I quiet myself in devotion. I breathe the world out and I breathe you in. Sadness lingers at times, but you fill me up with strength. You carry me through and deliver me into the next chapter. At this time, that story remains unwritten, but I wait in joyful hope for the promise of your kingdom.

Amen

April 28

"...'It is not the healthy who need a doctor, but the sick. I have not come to call the righteous, but sinners to repentance.'" Luke 5:31-32

Dear Lord,

Your love is medicine to my soul. You heal my troubles and restore me to health. I do not have the answers. I lay myself at your feet each day and open my heart to your guidance and correction. You straighten my path when I acknowledge your reprimand.

My imperfections are many. You love me because of how desperately I need you. The temptations of the world are many. No one can rightly walk this road alone. It is too easy to get pulled off course. You avail yourself to all who humbly seek your spiritual medicine.

Thank you for saving this wretched soul, Oh Lord.

Amen

April 29

"But whoever is united with the Lord is one with him in spirit." 1 Corinthians 6:17

Dear Lord,

I take this time with you today in quiet devotion and I seek you. The loving community that surrounds me unites me with the light of your love. You satisfy my needs as I commune with you. You breathe light into the darkened recesses of my soul.

As I breathe you in, I have light to pass to another. I cannot hoard your goodness, light or love. Those are gifts that are meant to be shared so all can be united in love. The loving light of the spirit is an end to suffering. No one needs to trudge this path alone.

Amen

April 30

"But thanks be to God! He gives us the victory through our Lord Jesus Christ." 1 Corinthians 15:57

Dear Lord,

The power of your spirit lives in me today. When I am struggling and wavering, I can quiet myself and you speak through me. When I am in right alliance with your spirit, you help fight the demons that could attack me.

With your help, Oh Lord, I am discovering my voice. My silent knowing that I have been talked out of my whole life is growing and gaining life. Through this indwelling I carve out a place for me to safely be in this world, insulated from further attack.

Although I once was lowly and insignificant, I am now mighty with your power. I am blessed to call you my Lord. You are a gracious and glorious Lord.

Amen

May 1

"Pay attention and turn your ear to the sayings of the wise, apply your heart to what I teach" Proverbs 22:17

Dear Lord,

As I drift through life it is easy to wander off course. I start to become overconfident and self-reliant at times. Praise to you today for how you make your teachings manifest in my life over the noise of the world. As I tune into you each day, I invite you in and you enter my soul. You guide me and direct me.

When I am not directly in tune, I have the resource of counsel that I am able to seek. Blessings to you today for this community surrounding me that helps me right my course when I get off track. As I return to you, you always embrace me.

Glory to you today, Oh Lord, as you renew me and redirect me.

Amen

May 2

"Submit yourselves, then, to God. Resist the devil, and he will flee from you." James 4:7

Dear Lord,

I lay myself at your feet today. I pour out self and I open myself to receive the light of your instruction. You want me to open my heart today. You want me to love and embrace those struggling around me and not to shut them out because of their differences.

Each of us has a story to tell. Although we may appear on the outside as though we fit a mold, each of us suffers uniquely with our own difficulties. I obey your commands today to the best of my abilities. I open myself to the least of my brothers and sisters. I welcome those who disconnect and isolate in fear to participate in the loving community here. There is a safe space within you; a holy, sacred temple of the Holy Spirit.

Amen

May 3

"There are different kinds of service, but the same Lord."
2 Corinthians 12:6

Dear Lord,

I give thanks to you today for the uniqueness of your creation. You have blessed each one of us with our own individual gifts. We are all called to serve according to how those gifts have been distributed. I am not a good singer, Lord. But I sing your praises through my writing.

My prayer today is that we could all allow ourselves to be different. I pray that we could stop trying to fit a mold and honor our calling in the kingdom of Christ. There is a place for everyone. Gifts have been disbursed to all. A good shepherd helps cultivate talent and reaps an abundant crop of gifted servants.

Amen

May 4

"I meditate on your precepts and consider your ways."
Psalm 119:15

Dear Lord,

I listen closely today for your direction. I quiet my mind and open my heart for your commands. Each day presents challenges that threaten to throw me off course. I take this time in the morning each day to review my plans for the day, and to include you in my activities.

It is easy for me to forget to do that during the day, Oh Lord. When I do not clear a path for your spirit to flow in, I can get sidetracked. I commit to follow in your ways to the best of my ability today and to keep my eyes on the prize of your kingdom. I will do my best to turn my thoughts to godly concerns and not to those of this earth, Oh Lord.

Amen

May 5

"Dear friends, let us love one another, for love comes from God. Everyone who loves has been born of God and knows God." 1 John 4:7

Dear Lord,

Thank you for those you have put into my life today, Oh Lord. I am surrounded by genuine love and community. Through this free exchange I come to know you and experience you on a deep, soul level.

We are all invited to commune in this way. Each one of us has something to give and receive if we are able to let go of our own egos long enough. Blessings and honor pour out from the cup of your love and you allow me to participate in your kingdom today as a whole person.

Please help us to lift one another up in your light until the end of days.

Amen

May 6

"Be kind and compassionate to one another, forgiving each other, just as Christ God forgave you." Ephesians 4:32

Dear Lord,

Please help me to always remember to practice lovingkindness toward my fellows today. Some days I am sensitive. My feelings can get hurt or I can feel resentful. I lay all of that at your feet today, Oh Lord. Please teach me how to let go of old hurts.

Please help me to learn to be like you, dear Lord; to begin anew with my community in the face of disappointments. We are all human. Each of us falls short each day. I cannot hold my family and friends up to a standard that I cannot keep myself.

No one of us is perfect. Certainly not me. I love and honor you today, Oh Lord, for how you have forgiven me. Please help me to remember to carry this forward.

Amen

May 7

"The Lord looks down from heaven on all mankind to see if there are any who understand, any who seek God." Psalm 14:2

Dear Lord,

You are my constant companion. I am never alone as you are always with me. You see all that takes place in your kingdom. You know all; everything about me. When I feel as though I am struggling alone, you are there. All I need to do is to reach out to you and you are there.

You send just the right people into my life today. You provide just the right inspiration and guidance. Although I may feel lowly and insignificant, I matter in your kingdom. We all matter. You call each of us to our own individual purpose. All we need to do is earnestly seek your calling.

Amen

May 8

"We do not want you to become lazy, but to imitate those who through faith and patience inherit what has been promised." Hebrews 6:12

Dear Lord,

I hear you calling today. I do not rest on my laurels, content with how I stayed focused yesterday. Each day begins anew with a chance for a fresh start, but also with new challenges and difficulties. As a runner trains each day for an upcoming race, we need to strengthen and grow our spiritual lives.

Sometimes I want to skip over the trials that present themselves. I want to throw in the towel or find an easier way. Today I connect with faith and patience regarding your promise for deliverance.

Your kingdom is now, Oh Lord. Your loving embrace is available here on earth. I turn to you today, Oh Lord, not to the comforts of the earth.

Amen

May 9

"But the fruit of the Spirit is love, joy, peace, forbearance, kindness, goodness, faithfulness, gentleness and self-control." Galatians 5:22

Dear Lord,

I invite the Spirit in. I breathe out selfishness and fear and I invite you in. Please light up my soul and ignite my fire. Please cultivate in me the fruits of the Spirit. Please help me to nourish and cultivate that heavenly place within my heart for you each day.

You call us, Oh Lord, to be a light in a darkened world. Please help me to be a cultivator of goodness in the lives of others. Just as you have sent your saints to me to witness truth, help me also to witness truth. Help me to be willing and able to hear your call.

Oh Lord, you bring joy amidst the suffering. You bring peace as I continually seek to walk in your way.

You are goodness and grace, Oh Lord.

Amen

May 10

"No discipline seems pleasant at the time, but painful. Later on, however, it produces a harvest of righteousness and peace for those who have been trained by it." Hebrews 12:11

Dear Lord,

Your love is like a perfect parent. When I am in abeyance with your commands, you abundantly reward me. When I get into self-centeredness or fear-based decision making, you provide correction. Many of us have a negative view of discipline based on life experience.

I know now, Lord, that you discipline me because you love me. You want me to experience the lessons in my missteps. You do not take your love away from me. I pull myself away from you when I get into my bad behaviors.

You call me when I am in the wilderness. You light my path when I get off track. You are a perfect parent. I embrace your corrections today, Oh Lord.

Amen

May 11

"But let all those who take refuge in you be glad; let them ever sing for joy. Spread your protection over them, that those who love your name may rejoice in you." Psalm 5:11

Dear Lord,

I seek shelter in you today. You protect me from the suffering of this world and you bring me comfort and joy. Your love is unfailing. I can always return to you. There are many voices now that can pull me away, that can make me angry and fearful.

We live in trying times, Oh Lord. It is easy to get discouraged. The balance of power is shifting. You pull me toward your guidance and love. Please shower your loving care over all of the earth. Please shine your light onto all who suffer, Lord.

Amen

May 12

"The Lord gives strength to his people; the Lord blesses his people with peace." Psalm 29:11

Dear Lord,

I am empty of self today. I let go of my fear and anxiety and I allow you to strengthen me. You quiet my mind and bring peace to my soul. Each day new challenges arise. I made time this morning to lay them at your feet.

Please guide my thoughts, words and actions today. Help me to be a carrier of peace to others who are in spiritual unrest. I seek to keep in right alignment with your directions so that I can maintain my inner calm and clarity. You are a blessed savior, Lord. Each morning I have a new opportunity to lay my troubles and misdeeds at your feet and begin anew.

I thank you for your presence in my life today. You breathe light into the darkness. Only you can fill the void within.

Amen

May 13

"'For the Son of Man came to seek and save the lost.'" Luke 19:10

Dear Lord,

When I was floating through life, lost and alone, you found me. Your way and your truth were witnessed to me by the most unlikely sources. I discovered more truth wherever I went when I was ready. You found me and you approached me on my level.

Each day, my Lord, I am lost without you. When I begin or end my day without your council I can feel that I am off-course. Today I seek you. Please help me to remember, as I go through this day, to take a moment before each impulse and to explore whether each action brings me closer to you or creates separation.

When I am close to you, Oh Lord, my soul feels delighted.

Amen

May 14

"Therefore each of you must put off falsehood and speak truthfully to your neighbor, for we are all members of one body." Ephesians 4:25

Dear Lord,

Please allow your spirit to enter me and fill me with your truth. Please give me the strength today to speak up and let my voice be heard. I need to love the sinner and hate the sin. I need to use my voice and all of the tools you have given me to ward off swords coming at me by hurt people living in the shackles of sin.

I lean into you today, Oh Lord. I lean into your goodness and truth. I recoil from the sin that tempts me today. We all have a voice that needs to be heard. We all need to advocate for ourselves and teach others to love us in ways that honor you and your kingdom.

I open myself to you, Oh Lord to hear your commands.

Amen

May 15

"Do not be afraid or terrified because of them, for the Lord your God goes with you; he will never leave you."
Deuteronomy 31:6

Dear Lord,

When I feel that hole inside my soul, your Word fills me up. There are many difficulties and challenges that present themselves. I think we all have weak moments. I know I do. I start to feel as though I am alone or abandoned; that I am incapable of some task that I am called to do.

Your love has always carried me through. When I give it over to you, you take away the fear and the isolation. Your love surrounds me when I allow it. You always avail yourself to me when I call upon you, Lord. You give me my close community that takes my burdens on as their own in support.

I still have to fight my own battles, but the armor of your love is all I need today.

Amen

May 16

"Since you are my rock and fortress, for the sake of your name lead me and guide me." Psalm 31:3

Dear Lord,

You provide shelter to me from the storms of life. I come to you today, I surrender myself to you. I open my heart to you so that you may provide guidance and direction. There are so many opportunities each day to stray off course. My pride, my fears and selfishness can take over in an instant.

I open myself to you, to the guiding force of your Spirit. I allow myself to feel and to let you ease my troubles and doubts. So long as I follow your guidance I have nothing to fear. I am never alone or left out in the cold, as long as I remember to invite you in.

You step in as pain, anger, fear and selfishness walk out. You comfort me and set my soul on fire, Oh Lord.

Amen

May 17

"When I am afraid, I put my trust in you," Psalm 56:3

Dear Lord,

So many worldly concerns run through my mind. I think about health issues, financial issues, lost relationships and past traumas. Sometimes I stay awake at night with these things on my heart. As I review my life, you have carried me through many pains and sufferings. You have been my deliverer and constant companion.

There is no reason for me to fear you as you are my Lord. I put my trust in you today and I know that you will grant me victory over strongholds in my life. I fight the daily battle of the human condition. So long as I walk in your ways and strive each day to be closer to you, you protect me. I surrender myself to you today that you may work in and through me.

Amen

May 18

"Produce fruit in keeping with repentance." Matthew 3:7

Dear Lord,

You have welcomed me to redemption time and time again. You have accepted my repentances and invited me to rejoin your community. Each time you offer corrections for me I better myself and strengthen my relationship with you. I remain open today to hear your calling.

Please help me to be able to offer the same type of love to others I encounter. Please help me not to engage in retaliation or argument, or to harbor resentments. Please grant me divine pause so that I may respond carefully and allow for teachable moments. Withdrawal from a relationship for a period is also a way of allowing healing.

Thank you for your loving insight and please help me always to continue to seek.

Amen

May 19

"Opponents must be gently instructed, in the hope that God will grant them repentance leading them to a knowledge of the truth" 2 Timothy 2:25

Dear Lord,

I come to your refuge today so that you may speak your truth into me. As teaching moments continue to present themselves, please help me to be tender yet firm in delivering my message. Please help me to speak in love and not in fear.

I feel your comfort and care today. I feel capable of transmitting your love and of teaching your way. I must fortify myself today through instruction in order to maintain my own humility and capability. Transgression comes from brokenness and separation from you. Right alignment with your way restores wholeness in communion with you and other fellow believers.

I open my arms today to all who seek correction and truth.

Amen

May 20

"Be devoted to one another in love. Honor one another above yourselves." Romans 12:10

Dear Lord,

I surrender myself today to your fellowship. I empty myself now of ego, pride, self-pity and fear. I take up service to my brothers and sisters. No one is alone in community and there is no greater honor than being called to service.

Our world honors the ego. Pride is revered here. In heavenly realms, it is good and right to be others-centered. Shifting my focus immediately quiets the mental chatter of needing to do, of needing to have, of needing to be anything other than alert in the present moment. In the present moment, service opportunities abound.

I am vibrantly alive each moment that I devote to my fellows. As I continue to reach outside of myself, you grow me more and more in your likeness.

Amen

May 21

"Rescue those being led away to death; hold back those staggering toward slaughter." Proverbs 24:11

Dear Lord,

I know you love me today. However, I am still completely human and imperfect. At times my course is unclear. I might falter or waiver in confusion. Despite how the world pulls at me and vies for my attention, I continue to seek you. I persevere.

We are all imperfect. Each one of us gives way to the world at one point or another. I know my calling, though, Lord. You have a job for me in your kingdom. There is a place for all of us in your kingdom.

You are gracious, Oh Lord, in how you whisper ever so gently to each one of us.

Amen

May 22

"The Lord is not slow in keeping his promise, as some understand slowness. Instead he is patient with you, not wanting anyone to perish, but everyone to come to repentance." 2 Peter 3:9

Dear Lord,

I come to you each morning in repentance. Each day I live an imperfectly human life. I surrender to you, Oh Lord. I give you my doubts, fears, pride and self-pity. I ask you to replace them with conviction, faith, humility and gratitude.

You are new each morning and you give me another chance. I have an opportunity today to grow more in your likeness and to move further away from my worldly ways. Mold me and shape me today. Help me to grow in your likeness more and more each day.

Amen

May 23

"'But store up for yourselves treasures in heaven, where moths and vermin do not destroy, and where thieves do not break in and steal." Matthew 6:20

Dear Lord,

I am a human being. My place is in the world. Yet please help me to be able to discern between heavenly involvements and material gains. Some relationships, although they may seem to nurture the soul, are distractions from the ultimate goal of rest and peace in your kingdom.

If relationships bring angst, trouble or worry to my spirit, that is an indicator that they do not fit with your will for my life. Whereas it is my job to do your work to seek and save the lost, it is also my responsibility not to be pulled off course. I cannot travel too far away from the lifeboat of your care, yet I myself become lost.

Allow me to be a beacon of your light, Oh Lord.

Amen

May 24

"Cherish her, and she will exalt you; embrace her and she will honor you." Proverbs 4:8

Dear Lord,

Let me always cherish wisdom. Help me to seek it, at all costs. I humble myself before you today as I let go of my ego and pride and invite in heavenly knowing. It is only through your God-consciousness that wisdom's truth can be embraced.

As I open my heart, I am honored and blessed. Divine insight can enter in in this manner and I can become a conduit of your light and love to others who might be floundering in darkness. There is a way out. There is a way to commune with grace and peace. I cherish the wisdom of your ways. Although I began in wretchedness, I am blessed by your grace.

Amen

May 25

"And the peace of God, which transcends understanding, will guard your hearts and your minds in Christ Jesus." Philippians 4:7

Dear Lord,

My faith in you today brings me comfort and care. My human intellect cannot comprehend all of your ways. You remain mysterious yet you are constant and abundant in love. You protect me and soothe my busy mind. In you, there is nothing to worry about as you will deliver me from my trials, as long as I put you first.

Please help me to remember to abandon myself to you each day. My desire is for you and your kingdom, not earthly trifles such as worry, doubt, fear and anxiety. You offer me so much more. Your comfort and care is available to all who heed the call.

You beckon us heavenward, Oh Lord. May I allow your peace in my heart.

Amen

May 26

"For lack of guidance a nation falls, but victory is won through many advisors." Proverbs 11:14

Dear Lord,

Your love is mighty. Your Word is a beacon of light. When I need direction beyond that, I seek you in prayer. I lay my cares at your feet. You are a good and gracious Lord, I also have a strong community of fellows who hear my troubles and breathe light into the darkness.

I have learned from my own experience, Lord, that I cannot do this life on my own. I need you and a community of believers to surround me and carry me in the right direction. As I move closer to you, others who honor your grace heed the call and envelop me in loving care.

I am open to receive you today, Oh Lord. You still speak if I can quiet myself to hear.

Amen

May 27

"Is anyone among you in trouble? Let them pray. Is anyone happy? Let them sing songs of praise." James 5:13

Dear Lord,

I pour myself out to you today. I ask you to protect me and to care for me in my earthly struggles. You know them all and I ask that you work in me and through me to overcome my difficulties. I want to witness your greatness and power as you work through your earthly servants.

I am grateful today as your love is unfailing. Even on difficult days when I feel as though I am unworthy, you open your arms to me and embrace me. You see me through good times and bad and you keep me on course. You are a life force that is open to all.

Amen

May 28

"Do not let any unwholesome talk come out of your mouths, but only what is helpful for building others up according to their needs, that it may benefit the Holy Spirit of God, with whom you were sealed for the day of redemption."
Ephesians 4:29

Dear Lord,

Many thoughts go through my mind each day. I am human, I lose my patience or get upset. Please help me to remember, Oh Lord, the power of words today. Please help me to take that pause before I speak. Help my words to build up, not tear down.

When I am feeling triggered by people, places and things, please help me to use restraint. My role is as a teacher. I am of no use to anyone if I allow myself to get pulled into the boxing ring. There is goodness, there is light, there is love. Let me remain connected to that so as to be patient and kind in instruction.

Amen

May 29

"I am not saying this because I am in need, for I have learned to be content whatever circumstances." Philippians 4:11

Dear Lord,

I endure many trials. Our world has much conflict and turmoil. You have brought me out of the darkness and connected me with the light of your spirit. The joy of your love is available at all times and far exceeds passing fancies.

You are constant and unfailing. When I let go of worldly concerns and pour out my heart to you, you fill me with your comfort and care. As I continue to seek you, you strengthen me so that others suffering in the dark may find light. Each one of your servants are meant to carry your message to a darkened world. A message of hope reigns supreme; a message of light.

Call forth those who suffer today. Let them lay their burdens at your feet so their hearts may sing your praises.

Amen

May 30

"You will be his witness to all people of what you have seen and heard." Acts 22:15

Dear Lord,

You have called me out of the darkness of this world. You have saved me from the shackles of addiction and toxic relationships. You have blessed me with a new life in which I can take a leadership role.

Only you are capable of that type of transformation. Only you can save us from this fallen world. You love me in my brokenness and you use me in ways I never thought possible. All you ask in return is my humility and discipleship. I follow in your ways, Oh Lord, as best I can. I carry your message to those who seek.

Your love is unfailing and your grace abounds.

Amen

May 31

"for all have sinned and fall short of the glory of God."
Romans 3:23

Dear Lord,

I humble myself before you today. I bring all my worldly cares and concerns. You know my true heart and my inherent human nature. I fortify myself in you, so that you may deliver me from my struggles. I seek your comfort and care today, Oh Lord, not the recognition of the world.

Please help me to be patient and kind with others today. Help me to remember that all of us struggle with being in bondage to natural instincts. There is no better or worse transgression, Oh Lord. All sin blocks us off from your glory.

I continue to turn away and shift my sights on you once more. Your grace abounds.

Amen

June 1

"Each one should test their own actions. Then they can take pride in themselves alone, without comparing themselves to someone else." Galatians 6:5

Dear Lord,

I often look around me at how others present their lives with jealousy. I long to escape my burdens and cares. Each one of us has our own troubles. Help me to simplify today. Help me to turn my sights on you. You have evidenced that you will provide genuine community.

There are those who coexist with me in brotherly communion and those who deplete me. I do not need to live a glamorous life. I do not need a high-profile lifestyle or to be the center of attention. I desire your comfort and care and a small circle of friends who provide reciprocal support.

You know my heart, Oh Lord. You know who belongs in my life. I surrender myself wholly to you.

Amen

June 2

"Love is patient, love is kind. It does not envy, it does not boast, it is not proud." 1 Corinthians 13:4

Dear Lord,

Please help me to always seek your divine light in all of my relationships. I lay all of my worldly desires at your feet. I surrender trying to control others. May I actively listen to the troubles of others (when they confide in me.) May I trust and not be fearful and jealous.

When I fix my sights on you, my loving relationships naturally fall into place. I can combat conflict by laying my troubles at your feet. When I clear my mind and wait for you to speak to me, you do so in your time.

I need to let go of my human urge to grasp and cling. You alone are my lifeline. I humble myself to you and allow your love to enter my heart.

Amen

June 3

"Jesus Christ is the same yesterday and today and forever."
Hebrews 13:8

Dear Lord,

In this modern world of constant change, only one thing remains the same; that is your unfailing love. I may feel at times that your love has moved or has been taken away. What instead has happened is that I have been pulled more toward the cares of the world and further from your grace.

I lean into your love today, Oh Lord. I ground myself in you. I let my community form around my relationship to you. I do not allow anyone or anything to come between my connection to you. When I put you first, everything else falls into place.

Amen

June 4

"Does wisdom not call out? Does not understanding raise her voice?" Proverbs 8:1

Dear Lord,

I begin today in quiet solitude with you. I empty myself of pride and ego and I invite in your loving spirit. As we sit quietly together, you give answers and help me to understand life's troubles. I take time to let your presence wash over me and I drink you in.

Please help me to always remember to carve out this sacred time. Your presence is the calm in the eye of the storm. I am merely human, Lord. I try not to allow myself to get caught up in the business of the world. All of that is mere distraction. Wisdom lies here, with you. It lies in the sanctuary of your presence.

I invite you into my heart today. The truth of your presence brings wisdom, understanding and joy.

Amen

June 5

"'It is when a person walks at night that they stumble, for they have no light.'" John 11:10

Dear Lord,

You light my path today. You provide wisdom, guidance and hope. When I was lost, I wandered alone in the darkness. I became ensnared by dark forces. We live in a time of intense spiritual warfare. I still struggle in my search for truth, but you call me onward like a beacon in the night.

Light my path today, Oh Lord. I stumble each day. I live an imperfect human life. As I increase my connection with you, the path becomes clearer. I encounter fellow travelers who make the journey more enjoyable. I learn today from your teachings. I improve from one day to the next. Though my body may weaken with age, my light grows stronger.

This light is available to all who earnestly seek.

Amen

June 6

"'In your anger do not sin' Do not let the sun go down while you are still angry, and do not give the devil a foothold." Ephesians 4:26

Dear Lord,

As I journey through life, I do have instances where I find myself getting upset. People rub me the wrong way, or push my buttons. Especially in close relationships, there are often points of contention. Differences of opinion can escalate quickly. I can harbor grudges and resentments with my fellows.

Please Lord, help me to soften my heart. Help me to forgive and to allow others the space to be who they need to be. If I hurt or offend, please help me to promptly be willing to make peace. Help me never to respond in retaliation even when angry. Please help me to keep my soul connection with you pure. Let me be able to privately retreat into my safe space to pray when I am troubled in my relationships.

I pray that I may bring your healing love to my troubled relationships today, Oh Lord.

Amen

June 7

"Hatred stirs up conflict, but love covers all wrongs."
Proverbs 10:12

Dear Lord,

We live in a conflicted world. We divide ourselves into camps and live in opposition with one another. Please Lord, help me to always invite your love in and let hatred flee from my heart. It is easy to repeat generational behaviors. Sometimes we adopt beliefs handed down without question.

I open my heart today to self-examination. I take an introspective approach and look within in response to hatred and resentment. Is there something within me that I can change to invite harmony? Is there something about my character that is fearful? For the basis of hate is fear.

May I form strong relations today. May my relationships be based on your love. May they grow, expand and help blot out hatred.

Amen

June 8

"In him was life, and that life was the light of all mankind."
John 1:4

Dear Lord,

You give life to my soul. You shine your light in my heart and make me a beacon to the lost. Each day I turn to you, for you to fill my heart with your words and your ways. I empty myself today and ask that you continue to fill my cup. Your love is sustenance.

This life force; this soul light is available to all. You cultivate goodness in all who allow you into their lives. Please continue to instruct me daily on how to walk more in your way. Guide me, teach me, illuminate my path. As I come nearer to you each day, you reveal yourself more and more. My purpose and mission are becoming clearer.

Please guide me and direct the world today. We need you now.

Amen

June 9

"He will take pity on the weak and the needy and save them from death." Psalm 72:13

Dear Lord,

I need you more and more each day. I come to you in weakness and you fortify me, you make me strong and you deliver me. I cannot handle the ways of this world without you. You give me peace and you take the worldly cares from my heart.

You are available to all who cry out for you, Lord. You fortify us and give peace to the troubled. When death comes, you give solace to those who claim you in their hearts. I turn my life to you, Oh Lord. In return you provide safety and abundance.

You are Lord of my life. Without you I am lost.

Amen

June 10

"So we fix our eyes not on what is seen, but on what is unseen, since what is seen is temporary, but what is unseen is eternal." 2 Corinthians 4:18

Dear Lord,

I come to you today, I carve out my quiet time. I ask that you help me to always remember to prioritize and to put you first. The material world offers many distractions. There are so many bright, flashy things that can grab my attention and pull me off course. I come to you each day, Oh Lord, so that you may fortify me and strengthen me.

Please help me to continue to develop that inner knowing of where true treasure lies. It is not in flashy looking people and things. It is in the simplicity and calm of rest in your presence. I lay my worldly cares at your feet. I know you will deliver me, oh Lord. I fix my sights on you today.

Guide me, direct me, lead me closer to you each day, Oh Lord.

Amen

June 11

"So then, let us not be like others, who are asleep, but let us be awake…" 1 Thessalonians 5:6

Dear Lord,

I keep my eyes wide open today to see the signs of your presence. You are all around me. Please help me to stay awake and present and not to fall off course. There are so many things to distract me in this modern world. There are so many ways of numbing the spiritual discomfort; so many ways of ignoring soul sickness.

I invite you into my pain today, Oh Lord. I do not seek to numb it. I choose healing today instead of harm. I breathe in the light of your love and breathe out hate and mistrust. You are all goodness and love. Your love connects us to each other and illuminates darkness.

I remain alert today to hear your call. I work to shine your message upon the world.

Amen

June 12

"Those who trust in themselves are fools, but those who walk in wisdom are kept safe." Proverbs 28:26

Dear Lord,

I empty myself to you today. I pour out selfish concerns and fill myself with your words and your ways. I make time for meditation today and time to come to you in prayer. I do this so that you may fill me up with your wisdom and guidance. Your commands are simple and your rewards are great.

You speak light to my soul. You quiet the chatter of my mind as I pour out my worldly concerns unto you. You align me with my community and nourish me. You do not take my difficulties, but you carry me through them. You are all I need. Through my connection with you, everything else in my life comes into focus.

You light my way, Oh Lord, and you guide my path.

Amen

June 13

"Let the wise listen and add to their learning, and let the discerning get guidance –" Proverbs 1:5

Dear Lord,

I open my channels to hear your voice. I bring my struggles to you in prayer and you speak to my heart. No matter what the situation, you provide guidance and clarity. Sometimes I need to seek guidance for months or even years before I get answers. In time, you make your ways known if I continue to seek each day.

Many times I try to take matters into my own hands. I try to solve my own problems instead of turning them over to your loving care. You inevitably get my attention. Some of the lessons have been difficult. They have not been to my liking. They are to the benefit of my spiritual growth if I become willing to allow you to direct me.

I turn myself over to you today, Oh Lord. I come to you in search of your kingdom.

Amen

June 14

"For this is the message you heard from the beginning: We should love one another." 1 John 3:11

Dear Lord,

You have been clear in your message. You have instructed me to blot out the hate in my heart. I come to you today, I pour out my struggles, and you fill me with your commands. You abhor bitterness and resentment. Your truth in this regard has been clear from the beginning. There have been times, in my spiritual immaturity, that I have resisted this.

May I allow my heart to soften today. May I see each person as your divine creation, broken in their humanness as they may be. May I remain humble and not judge others who may not have pursued the path to wholeness just yet. Please guide and instruct my behavior so that I do not chastise.

We are all unique, Lord. Each of us has a calling. May I not find mine at the expense of others.

Amen

June 15

"He has made everything beautiful in its time. He has also set eternity in the human heart; yet no one can fathom what God has done from beginning to end." Ecclesiastes 3:11

Dear Lord,

As I draw nearer to you, you ignite the beauty in my soul. This is available to all who seek. Where darkness once abounded, you have brought beauty and light. You call us toward you. May we be open and willing to hear the call.

Your love is timeless and your true community is eternal. There comes in time an inner knowing. In my human condition I cannot understand or explain all of your ways. I don't comprehend how but I have faith today that if I do my best to keep your commands, great rewards will be provided in kind.

Today I put my faith in you, Lord. I fix my sights on your unseen kingdom.

Amen

June 16

"God is faithful, who has called you into fellowship with his Son, Jesus Christ our Lord." 1 Corinthians 1:9

Dear Lord,

You beckon me toward you today. You call me to leave behind my worldly cares and relationships and commune with you. As I let go of old relations, you bring into my life those who are the perfect fit for my life. As long as I seek and follow you, I will attract genuine fellowship to me.

Like-minded folk attract one another. Let me be willing to make a leap of faith and leave behind toxic, worldly relationships. For once I free up that space in my life, I allow for true community with my authentic self and your people.

I allow you into my life today, Lord. I set aside toxicity and invite authenticity. I put my faith in you, Lord.

Amen

June 17

"Praise the Lord, all his heavenly hosts, you his servants who do his will." Psalm 103:21

Dear Lord,

You know my true heart. You hear my confessions and know my shortcomings. I am a human creation with many flaws. Each day I seek you though, Oh Lord. I draw near to you and listen to your call. I study your Word and take it into my soul.

I do my best to obey your commands. I approach all I come into contact with with love and tolerance. I lay my life at your feet and open myself up to be a vessel of your works. I believe and I surrender my will and my life to your ways. I confess my sins and repent. I make reparations for harms I have done when needed. I work to forgive those who have hurt me.

Your yoke is easy, Lord. If I remind myself each day to stop trying to control and let you take the reins.

Amen

June 18

"I gave you milk, not solid food, for you were not yet ready for it." 1 Corinthians 3:2

Dear Lord,

When we are new creations in your Word, we come to you like babies. We do not understand the fullness of the message. It may frighten and intimidate us. I will stay in the present moment today, Lord. I will focus on how you speak to me each day about my troubles.

I pour out my heart to you and I do my best to hear you speak to me. Love is mother's milk to us as new believers. You call us into abounding love and grace. You forgive us, you forget our wrongdoings, you give us a second chance to embrace goodness and righteousness, regardless of our backgrounds. As we mature in faith our understanding will increase.

Amen

June 19

"My message and my preaching were not with wise and persuasive words, but with a demonstration of the Spirit's power" 1 Corinthians 2:4

Dear Lord,

Your message has hit me the hardest when spoken through the most unlikely of vessels. Learned scholars generally speak over my head. When a believer pours out their true testimony in witness of your love, that is what speaks to me. When the downtrodden are lifted to greatness by the light of your love, that sets my soul on fire.

Each one of us, regardless of social status, race, national origin, etc. is capable of having a vital spiritual experience if we can soften our hearts to allow trust and love as a starting point. The message is simple and does not need to be consolidated. Love your God, love your fellows, do good works.

Amen

June 20

"He heals the brokenhearted and binds up their wounds."
Psalm 147:3

Dear Lord,

You are friend to all who cry out to you. Each morning I come to you in my brokenness and you fill my cup. You renew my spirit when I invite you into my darkness. You shine a light on my troubles and give me relief. When my spirits are low, you pick me up.

As I pour out my ego and self-centeredness and invite you in, your spirit speaks through me. You empower me and strengthen me. You give voice to the voiceless. You remind me that I matter. You remind me that my fellowship of like-minded friends care about me. You bring me out of isolation into your loving community. There I am fortified and validated. I am no longer alone.

You are a glorious and righteous Lord. You are worthy of praise.

Amen

June 21

"By wisdom a house is built, and through understanding it is established" Proverbs 24:3

Dear Lord,

I turn to your Word. I pour out my heart to you in prayer and I hear your still, small voice speak to me. Wisdom enters after a time and around that is built a spiritual foundation. Evidence has appeared in my life that has created an inner knowing.

This knowledge is the beginning of understanding. Your presence is something my human mind is incapable of fully understanding. It's a feeling in my soul. It is built on a track record that has been established as I have put my trust and faith in you, and have sought your ways. You lift me up. You bring peace and deliverance when I put you first. This spiritual house has room for all.

Learn and grow in knowledge. Search your soul for the truth that lies within.

Amen

June 22

"Let us come before him with thanksgiving and extol him with music and song." Psalm 95:2

Dear Lord,

I pour out my heart to you in gratitude today. You have provided for all of my needs. You have given me food, shelter, family and friends. I sing your praises and do your bidding. And you bless me abundantly. All I have and all that I am comes from you. You provide deliverance from my difficulties, Oh Lord, and the support of a loving community.

There have been hard times, Lord. There have been times of great difficulty when my faith has faltered. I have stumbled many times. Each time I turn back to you, you pick me up and set me back on course. I am grateful, Lord, that you do not demand perfection. You want all of me and I surrender myself to you today, Oh Lord.

Amen

June 23

"Now to each one the manifestation of the Spirit is given for the common good." 1 Corinthians 12:7

Dear Lord,

The light of your spirit lies within each one of us. It is up to me to nurture it and to strengthen it. As the firelight begins to shine brighter, I do not hoard it all for myself. I turn my attention outward to serve the kingdom. We feed off of each other, Lord. Genuine fellowship of the spirit is a foundation of growth.

You invite each one of us to grow and become stronger for the benefit of the whole. Corruption will tear down the community while humility, honesty and service will build it up. There is no hierarchy in your love. We are all on equal footing. If one has more, he gives more.

May the light of your love always enlarge us. May we lift each other up and not tear each other down.

Amen

June 24

"Devote yourselves to prayer, being watchful and thankful."
Colossians 4:2

Dear Lord,

I kneel before you today. I empty myself of fear, earthly desire and dishonesty. I invite you into my soul. You listen with care to my troubles. You provide guidance and direction. You shine your light into the darkened recesses of my soul as we commune.

I come to you in this manner each morning. I come to you when I want to, when I long to. I also come to you when I don't want to. I come to you and invite you in, even when I am caught up in self-will and am not wanting to surrender to your ways. I ask for the willingness and in time it comes.

I am so grateful today, Oh Lord, to have you as my best friend. You are my closest confidant and I don't need to explain or justify that.

My prayer and meditation is the building block of my day.

Amen

June 25

"For God did not appoint us to suffer wrath but to receive salvation through our Lord Jesus Christ." 1 Thessalonians 5:9

Dear Lord,

It has taken me many years to understand that you are not out to get me. You are not standing around waiting to condemn me. Every time I slip up, you are watching over me like a loving parent. You offer corrections when needed, however, if I am always seeking to walk in your ways, it is not difficult to right my course.

I open my heart today to receive your grace and forgiveness. I listen and study so that I may better understand your will for my life. Speak to my soul today as I invite you into my spirit. Breathe your truth into me and give me discernment so that I may steer clear of worldly temptation and immediate gratification.

Your graciousness abounds today, Lord. Great are you for your unfailing love.

Amen

June 26

"'Therefore I tell you, whatever you ask for in prayer, believe that you have received it, and it will be yours.'" Mark 11:24

Dear Lord,

You called me out of the darkness. In the pit of my despair, you gave me the ability to imagine myself as something more than what I was. You gifted me with the ability to dream. I prayed fervently requesting relief from my suffering and you have provided that.

The life I have today is the life I envisioned all those years ago. I was in the shackles of addiction, but today I walk free. I asked and it was given. I groveled at your feet; I poured out my heart to you and you have heard me. I still have so many struggles and I give them over to you, Oh Lord. You know my heart and you provide answers in your time and manner.

Amen

June 27

"For the love of money is a root of all kinds of evil. Some people, eager for money, have wandered from the faith and pierced themselves with many griefs." 1 Timothy 6:10

Dear Lord,

Help me always to remember to put you first. Whereas money is necessary in this life, it must not come before my relationship with you. When I put you first, everything else falls into place around that. I attract the right people, friends, the right job and the right community.

Chasing after money leads to insanity in the end. It is an empty, meaningless god. I seek a simple life with simple pleasures. I seek humility, love and gentleness. Those are the fruits of your kingdom. When I seek those things and do the footwork, money comes naturally. I don't have to stress or force anything. Everything flows.

Amen

June 28

"My soul thirsts for God, for the living God. When can I go and meet with God?" Psalm 42:2

Dear Lord,

I long to have you near me. I crave your presence. When you are close to me, others who crave your blessings surround me. In my human state, there are barriers that seep in that cause me to separate from you. I keep a constant watch to right my wrongs as soon as I am able.

Dwelling deeply in worldly affairs causes me a disturbance. Afer a time, my eating habits are affected, my sleep is affected and I find myself ill-tempered. Daily I come to you. I open my heart a little at a time and I allow you to shine your glorious light. Other fallen angels walk this path with me and, together, we draw nearer to you. I strive to have my soul cleansed so that in the end, I may dwell in your presence forever.

Amen

June 29

"but you give us victory over our enemies, you put our adversaries to shame." Psalm 44:7

Dear Lord,

Not too long ago, I was an angry, contemptuous soul. I was in a constant state of annoyance. I have followed your commands to the best of my ability and I have seen those who lived in opposition to me fall away. As I continue to work on molding myself more in your likeness, some former enemies become friends.

When we are shackled by the world, we do not see the truth. We look through the eyes of fear, envy and hatred. We become capable of loving even those who previously seemed unlovable, as we come closer to you. We command respect even from those we do not like. We become willing and able to forgive ourselves and others and that cultivates kindness.

Amen

June 30

"We want each of you to show this same diligence to the very end, so that what you hope for may be fully realized." Hebrews 6:11

Dear Lord,

I kneel at your feet today. I empty my heart to you. I search your Word. I write down my soul. You allow me to know the truth about you and about myself in a gentle and tender way. As I come closer to this truth, I find my voice. I speak up for myself and for what I need. I am heard.

I do not overstep my boundaries, Lord. If I do, I sincerely apologize, sometimes to the point of weeping. I find my place in your kingdom. I am made whole by doing so. I find my tribe with other seekers of your truth. We light each other's paths and you deliver us.

Amen

July 1

"Therefore, as we have opportunity, let us do good to all people, especially to those who belong to the family of believers." Galatians 6:10

Dear Lord,

Please help me to be a beacon of light to all who I encounter. You bless me, Oh Lord, with fellowship. The community around me, along with the joy of your love carry me through my difficulties. I bear witness to the fact that genuine community and love are available to all.

May we who believe not remain cloistered in the comfort of the church. May we reach out to those in need. May we extend ourselves to those who suffer. May we do what we can to mend the broken and to heal the wounded. For we are made whole only through your love and the body of Christ.

All glory and honor is yours this day Oh Lord.

Amen

July 2

"Choose my instruction instead of silver, knowledge rather than choice gold" Proverbs 8:10

Dear Lord,

I may work to adorn my body. I may labor to acquire wealth and material objects. If I do not nurture my soul all will be lost in the end. When our time comes, we return to you, alone. If we do not enlarge our spiritual lives in the time we are allotted, we will come to pass in despair.

May I devote myself daily to learning to follow you. May I add to my life only that which creates balance and harmony in my spirit. May I tune out all of the noise; eliminate the distractions. May I listen to the spirit whisper its truth. Your voice comes to me in stillness. I will find you when I can get quiet.

Amen

July 3

"Be kind and compassionate to one another, forgiving each other, just as in Christ God forgave you." Ephesians 4:32

Dear Lord,

You are good and gracious. You have cleansed me of the impunity of sin. Each day as I turn my imperfections over to you, your grace perseveres and I am washed clean once more. Help me to never sit above another soul in judgment, but to approach all as I would want to be treated.

I seek to obey your commands, Oh Lord, but each day I fall short. Each day I get up and study again to improve, to draw nearer to you. Let us as a body not hold onto grudges regarding the behavior of others. May we soften our hearts to forgive as you have; to gently instruct as you do. For some actions, we must be held accountable. The consequences are lessons, not punishments. All of life has value in your eyes. All souls are salvageable, if they have the capacity to love.

Amen

July 4

"Lord my God, I called to you for help, and you healed me."
Psalm 30:2

Dear Lord,

I was a wretched sinner. I was an addict and an alcoholic. I was enslaved by sin. I was held in the bondage of relationships that completely blocked my relationship to you. You intervened on my behalf. You called me out of the darkness. You restored my mind and my spirit.

You are a great healer, Oh Lord. Many professionals work as your servants without knowing it. I had medical professionals, pastors, priests, nuns and lay teachers who brought me back to life. I am a living witness of what your goodness can bring to the lives of the broken.

You are good and gracious, Oh Lord. Your love endures.

Amen

July 5

"Whoever conceals their sins does not prosper, but the one who confesses and renounces them finds mercy." Proverbs 28:13

Dear Lord,

May you continue to bless me with the gift of transparency. When I am struggling with temptation, I am hyper-aware of it. You reveal my shortcomings to me each day as I lay down my burdens and lift others up. I open myself to the community that surrounds me and admit my transgressions.

You continue to show me the path back to your favor, oh Lord. Prayer, meditating on your Word and gentle guidance from my trusted fellows shine a light in the darkness. There is always a way back to you, Oh Lord. Your grace and mercy forgive and reunite the broken, wounded and downtrodden.

Great is your mercy today, Oh Lord. Glory to you on high.

Amen

July 6

""You make known to me the path of life, you will fill me with joy in your presence, with eternal pleasures at your right hand." Psalm 16:11

Dear Lord,

You call me into a simple life. My days are quiet and are spent in your presence. I make myself available to those who seek council in much the same way you do for me so that I may give that to others.

There is joy in stillness. A peace comes in time that defies explanation. My eyes open to see the everyday beauty of the sunrise; to hear the songs of birds singing all around me. I am blessed today, Oh Lord, to have a purpose in your kingdom. I am honored to be among your creation.

Amen

July 7

"My son, pay attention to my wisdom, turn your ear to my words and insight." Proverbs 5:1

Dear Lord,

I open my heart to hear your message today. I bow at your feet in prayer. I give myself over to you. Please help my heart to soften to my fellows so that I may bear with them in tolerance. No one among us is perfect. We all have much to learn each day on our journey toward wholeness.

Each day I look to your Word to speak to me. You invariably provide guidance and direction. All you require is that I open my heart and earnestly seek. No one on earth is eternally severed from the light of your love. May all who desire, be reunited with you in the glory of your kingdom.

Amen

July 8

"I know that you are pleased with me, for my enemy does not triumph over me." Psalm 41:11

Dear Lord,

As I draw nearer to you each day, I gain more personal power. I am more effective at speaking my mind so that I may be heard. I do not let darkness and chaos invade my spirit so easily. The light does always triumph over the dark. The dark respects the light.

When I lay my brokenness at your feet, Oh Lord, you fortify and strengthen me. As I draw nearer to you each day, those who surround me see the shift and ask questions. Your truth is undeniable. There is strength in your love to rebuild, to overcome.

Amen

July 9

"There is no fear in love. But perfect love drives out fear, because fear has to do with punishment. The one who fears is not made perfect in love." 1 John 4:18

Dear Lord,

Please take away my fear. Today I breathe in the light of your love and breathe out fear. There is so much uncertainty in today's world. Disease, discord, social and political unrest; these can all weigh heavily on our hearts at times. It is easy for me to fall victim to the thought construct that you are punishing me and my culture.

When I invite love in, I am blessed with knowing. You come to instruct, not to punish. As I seek you more and more deeply each day, I find solace in that space. I find deep peace in tuning out the noise and inviting you in to love me. I make myself available to you today, in loving service.

Amen

July 10

"For we are co-workers in God's service; you are God's field, God's building." 1 Corinthians 3:9

Dear Lord,

You are a good and gracious Lord. You have blessed each and every one of us with many gifts. You call all of us to service based on those gifts. There is no right or wrong way to serve. We contribute when we listen to others. We contribute when we show we care. Those are simple ways of serving that can have a big impact.

We may come up against others who are quite insistent that we serve in a particular fashion. We need to trust our instincts if something feels wrong for us. Once we clear away the blocks to your light, we will know personal truth. You will light our paths and guide our way. We will find how we fit into your kingdom in a manner that is safe and that honors our whole person.

Amen

July 11

"The unfolding of your words gives light, it gives understanding to the simple." Psalm 119:130

Dear Lord,

I look to your Word today for guidance and direction. I open my heart to you so that you may speak to me. I tune in to my community and bring what you want. May I be a beacon of light and love.

For I know it is your wish that none be forsaken. Your message needs to be brought to the forgotten numbers. Your church struggles to meet the needs of the world. Your people are hurting. My lesson today is to allow my pain. My lesson is to feel it and move through it. My lesson is to nurture everyone with kindness and love. May we all be willing to open our hearts today and grow beyond the hurt.

Amen

July 12

"I will walk about in freedom, for I have sought your precepts." Psalm 119:45

Dear Lord,

Each day I come before you. I humble myself and open up to receive your commands. I do not follow your instructions perfectly, Oh Lord. No one does. However, by my willingness to follow you, I have been set free from the bondage of self. I am open and available to form genuine relationships with those I encounter.

You are a gracious Lord. This genuine human experience is available to all who seek to follow in your ways. You guide us toward authenticity. You guide us into real relations with you and with one another. May I always remember to be willing, Oh Lord, to put you first and from that connection, everything else falls into place.

Amen

July 13

"Each of you should use whatever gift you have received to serve others, as faithful stewards of God's grace in its various forms." 1 Peter 4:10

Dear Lord,

You have blessed each one of us with many gifts. No gift is more valuable than another, just as no one person has more value than another. May I work, Oh Lord, to help others to discover their gifts. May I work to help others to see that all have value in your kingdom.

There is no one right way to serve. There is no mold that we can fit into. Perhaps certain authority figures have pounded this into our heads and, for that reason, we feel certain that we will not be able to make a contribution. You nudge us out of this thought construct by your Word, Oh Lord. May we always seek your truth and not rely on others to tell us what to do.

Amen

July 14

"Do not lie to each other, since you have taken off your old self with its practices and have put on the new self." Colossians 3:9

Dear Lord,

There are many pressures and demands from this world. As someone who is a people pleaser, it is often difficult to balance the needs of everyone in my life. May I always strive to avoid nervous chatter as it is often a breeding ground for speculation and conjecture. May I also dive deeply into your Word and my prayer life, to continually seek your truth.

I want to achieve genuine authenticity. I desire to present myself consistently in a genuine way to everyone in my life. I get into trouble when I find myself trying to be different things to different people. My best defense against this is to find some solitude each day and to observe my thoughts. If I am continually being fake or putting on a charade, perhaps I need to make adjustments to my social circle.

Amen

July 15

"Like newborn babies, crave pure spiritual milk, so that by it you may grow up in your salvation" 1 Peter 2:2

Dear Lord,

As I am coming into alignment with a genuine relationship with you, please help me to seek out the invitation of your Word. I think that religion will often eliminate spirituality from its teachings. I have a religious practice that is uniquely my own. It may involve going to church and it may not; that depends on many factors.

I consult your Word regularly. I practice love above all and inclusion. If someone can commit verses to memory or preach doctrine, that is separate from the practice of spirituality. Your love, as outlined in the gospel, was to embrace; to gently guide and instruct. It was not to intimidate or overpower. For no one can get to the path of truth if they are condemned before being able to start.

Please help me to be willing, Lord, to take a step back if I am being led toward judgment. Please help others to do the same toward me.

Amen

July 16

"Whoever has ears, let them hear." Matthew 11:15

Dear Lord,

May all who can hear and process awaken to your message of redemption. The light of your love can heal us and uplift us. You call us into loving community with one another. You call us to respect and honor you through prayer and genuine fellowship.

May we not cultivate an exclusive faith. May we all learn to be more open, willing and tolerant of people. May we gently instruct and not egotistically rebut. We are all sinners, dear Lord. No one sin is greater than another. One command, however, comes first, your command to love others as ourselves. May I first seek to love and forgive others, thus achieving self-love and compassion.

Amen

July 17

"Do not conform to the pattern of this world, but be transformed by the renewing of your mind. Then you will be able to test and approve what God's will is – his good, pleasing and perfect will." Romans 12:2

Dear Lord,

May I be sober, awake and alert today to hear your commands. May I not seek to mold myself in the ways of the world, but to conform more to your ways. May I seek to always surround myself with people who appropriately, tenderly correct me. May I commune with like-minded fellows who instruct and encourage.

As I mold myself more in your likeness, I draw a different community into my life. If I can be willing to learn from others, I draw closer to your likeness. My life has become transformed in this manner. I am a new creation in you. I am no longer floundering around, cast adrift in a meaningless world. I have purpose and drive in my life.

Glory and honor to you, Oh gracious Lord.

Amen

July 18

"Cast but a glance at riches, and they are gone, for they will surely sprout wings and fly off to the sky like an eagle."
Proverbs 23:5

Dear Lord,

Money is a requirement to get through this life. May we not make it our master. When I put you first and devote my life to your humble service, you bless me with abundance. I am rich in community, rich in the light of your love.

Although I may have some financial obstacles in my way at this time, I maintain faith. I know that if I enlarge my spiritual life, I am storing up riches that will yield a financial result. All I ultimately need to do is the footwork and I know that you will provide. All of my needs are met today. I have the blessings of your love, the most valuable gift there is.

Amen

July 19

"How priceless is your unfailing love, O God! People take refuge in the shadow of your wings." Psalm 36:7

Dear Lord,

You are my comfort. You are my protector in times of trouble. Your love envelops me and eases my mind. You provide a safe haven. You shelter me from the storms of life. Yes, there are hard times. Some days my load feels heavy. My mind can spin or worry.

You ground me in the community of your love. As I seek my truth daily you bring forth like-minded fellows. When I cannot bear my burdens alone, I realize that I do not have to. I have companionship and support when I open myself up to it. My life is messy, Oh Lord. You meet me where I am. The beauty of your love shines through every time.

Amen

July 20

"In my distress I called out for the Lord; I cried to my God for help. From his temple he heard my voice; my cry came before him, into his ears." Psalm 18:6

Dear Lord,

In my suffering I have cried out to you. You do not take away the pain of life, however you comfort me. You walk with me on my journey as my constant companion. You send others into my life to support me as I do for them in kind.

You provide rest when I am weary. You are a safe haven in troubled times. Only you remain constant and unchanging in this uncertain world. You have known me since before I was born. I desire to return to you in a childlike fashion, wholly and blameless in your sight. Each day I seek to start anew; to walk more closely to you than the day before.

You are gracious and glorious in your way, Oh Lord.

Amen

July 21

"...He causes his sun to go down on the evil and the good, and sends rain on the righteous and the unrighteous."
Matthew 5:45

Dear Lord,

So many times in my social circles I have heard it said that good people receive blessings. Bad people receive punishment and trials. This has not been my life experience. My trials and struggles have been some of my greatest teachers. I have garnished so much wisdom from persevering through troubled times.

Those who have not been tested, have an immature faith. Anyone who grew up surrounded by the above-mentioned thought construct would naturally question or challenge their belief systems when enduring hardship. Let us all support each other through the deepest, soul- wrenching pain; through questions of faith or identity reconstruction.

God's truth is available to all. Not only a select few.

Amen

July 22

"Awake, and rise to my defense! Contend for me, my God and my Lord." Psalms 35:23

Dear Lord,

You know all of the intimate details of my life. I lay my troubles at your feet daily. I prostrate myself before you and request that you enter my life. I have come to you many times. I was empty and doubtful. I have begged and pleaded with you to take my burdens from me.

You do not always oblige me in this manner. When I repeatedly, religiously come before you and enter into a relationship, a shift begins to happen. You begin to work in me and through me. You enter into my life in a meaningful way and strengthen me so that I may be an overcomer. You cheer me on to fight my demons and achieve peace.

You are a good and gracious Lord.

Amen

July 23

"This only I have found; God created mankind upright, but they have gone in search of many schemes." Ecclesiastes 7:29

Dear Lord,

We are all born perfect in your love. As we mature in the ways of the world, temptation finds us. I am human. The world taunts me daily. We all, everyone of us, have our weaknesses that we battle against. I sin and I miss your mark of perfection each day.

As I strengthen my relationship with you, my faith matures. I learn what my hot buttons are and turn my shortcomings over to you daily. As I become more aware each day of my own set of imperfections, I learn how to better modify my behavior. I grow in your likeness more each day. Your grace abounds when I lapse back into my defects from time to time. I continue to slip, but the severity lessens over time.

You are a gracious and forgiving Lord, my God.

Amen

July 24

"He went into the country around the Jordan, preaching a baptism of repentance for the forgiveness of sins." Luke 3:3

Dear Lord,

I come before you today a lowly sinner. Each morning as I pour out my heart to you, I empty myself of my shortcomings and imperfections. You graciously embrace me and restore me to wholeness. You wipe my slate clean and provide an opportunity to learn from my mistakes and grow more in your likeness.

There have been times, Oh Lord, when I have believed that I have fallen too far to get up. There have been times that I have felt that I have gone too far astray to come back to your love. Let us bear in mind that no one sin is greater than another. We are all imperfect in our humanness. The glory is in the practice; the drive to grow closer to you, Oh Lord, day by day.

Amen

July 25

"Every good and perfect gift is from above, coming down from the Father of the heavenly lights, who does not change like shifting shadows." James 1:17

Dear Lord,

Our modern world moves at such a fast pace. We live in an ever-changing world, and it is difficult to find a place to grow roots. Friends and loved ones come and go, even jobs and everything in our economy can change in the blink of an eye.

You are the only thing that is constant, Oh Lord. You are steady and unmoving. There have certainly been times that I have not been standing on solid ground. That is not because you have moved, Oh Lord. It is because I have faltered in the diligence of my daily practice. May I always put you first, Oh Lord. May I remember to let everything else fall into place around my relationship to you.

Amen

July 26

"Whatever you do, work at it with all your heart, as working for the Lord, not for human masters" Colossians 3:23

Dear Lord,

Please ignite your spirit in all of my duties. As a mom, as a wife, as a recovery seeker, as a wellness practitioner, as a writer. May you work through me in each of these roles that I play. I think I sometimes get caught up in the world and the thought that it is only at work, in government, through achieving wealth and power that your ways are present.

I live simply and humbly. Yet I know that when I am grounded and centered in your love, you are able to work through me. May I be a vessel today that you can work through. Please rid me of pride and ego and allow me to receive and carry your message.

Amen

July 27

"Fools give full vent to their rage, but the wise bring calm in the end." Proverbs 29:11

Dear Lord,

May I be able to maintain my pause today. When I experience something that triggers an emotional reaction in me, may I be able to take a moment, breathe carefully in and out a couple of times and reply. Sometimes I may even need to turn around and walk away. I may need to revisit the topic or exchange at a later time.

These are all options that become available to me as I grow in your grace. In my immaturity everything was a knee-jerk reaction. I did not have that safe space in the seat of my soul in which to retreat. You have blessed me with this through the indwelling of your love that I refer to as the Holy Spirit. It also may be referred to as source, light or other similar names. This presence is available to all who earnestly seek.

Amen

July 28

"To all perfection I see a limit, but your commands are boundless." Psalm 119:96

Dear Lord,

Each one of us is imperfect. Regardless of how we may present ourselves or try to appear, we are all human and by nature we are flawed. You are the only perfection there is. May I strive to grow closer to you each day. May I study your Word and offer myself wholly to you each day.

As we grow in your love our imperfections will become minimized. We will become more like you. We will have strength to overcome where previously we did not. No one among us can achieve greatness, but we may become more polished. May I always seek to do your will. May I start each day with gratitude and humility. I am endlessly broken. I am only made whole by the light of your love.

Amen

July 29

"Your word is a lamp for my feet, a light for my path."
Psalm 119:105

Dear Lord,

I come to you so that you may speak to me. May I always remember to seek you each day. Although I was doubtful in the beginning, I have become faithful. Once I was wretched and now within me your light shines. I do not have a perfect understanding of your Word. I do not know what tomorrow may bring.

As I come to you daily however, in the darkness of my confusion, you slowly awaken me. I am becoming more assured of your plan for my life. You reveal yourself more each day. I do not get guidance solely by your written Word. You come to me in quiet prayer. You reveal yourself in dreams. I hear your guidance in the voice of wise counsel. You comfort me, Oh Lord. You provide me constant companionship.

Amen

July 30

"These are the people who divide you, who follow mere natural instincts and do not have the Spirit." Jude 1:19

Dear Lord,

Each one of us has natural instincts. Our instincts were given by you and are therefore inherently good. When I am not in tune with my indwelling spirit, I can let my instincts lead me off the path of wholeness. Once that happens, it becomes difficult to find the way back.

Oh Lord, please help me to seek you above all things. I invite the Holy Spirit to enter me and guide my decisions today; to move me toward the right action. As our culture moves away from spiritual grounding our instincts run riot. Please bring your light and guidance to us today, Oh Lord. Please guide us back.

Amen

July 31

"Instead we were like young children among you. Just as a nursing mother cares for her children" 1 Thessalonians 2:7

Dear Lord,

You are tender and gentle with me. You nurture my spirit when I seek to grow in your ways. When I get off course, you provide correction. I used to fear these corrections, it used to feel as though you were taking your love away from me.

I have a different understanding of your love today. As with a loving parent, when I do not get my way there are many reasons underlying it. It may be that what I wanted was not best for me. It may be my time to learn independence. The timing may not be right. The important thing is for me to make a beginning in trusting your greatness and infinite wisdom. I also need to recognize the limitations of my human understanding. We cannot see what you do, Oh Lord.

Amen

August 1

"he refreshes my soul, He guides me along the right paths for his name's sake." Psalm 23:3

Dear Lord,

As I walk nearer to you, you bring peace and quiet to my life. Where my day was once filled with noise, endless chatter, and constant drama, I seek quiet solitude and you meet me there. I invite others to commune in that space with me.

You provide love and care. You provide comfort and genuine community. Life is less busy now. There is less flash; less involvement in worldly concerns. Life is simpler, more genuine and wholesome. I make time for reading and studying. I sit and invite you. When I am genuinely empty of myself and my troubles, in time you come to me.

You are available to all, Oh Lord.

Amen

August 2

"If one of you says to them, 'Go in peace; keep warm and well fed,' but does nothing about their physical needs, what good is it?" James 2:16

Dear Lord,

May I be a person of action today. May I seek to serve the community around me. Simply offering up prayer and supplication is not what you desire. I need to be in the world, actively participating in the struggles of others. Instead of insulating myself in the cocoon of the church body, I need to be wholly immersed with your people.

May I always be willing to serve at this level. May I also not lose my faith or my connection in getting caught up in the pain of this world. May I feel deeply, then allow your strength to take over. We were not meant to shoulder our burdens alone. We should all support each other in genuine community.

Amen

August 3

"Do not be anxious about anything, but in every situation, by prayer and petition, with thanksgiving, present your requests to God." Philippians 4:6

Dear Lord,

As I come before you each day and surrender myself wholly to you, you replace doubt with faith. Sometimes I worry. I think I will not have enough money, that I will lose my position in the community or that my friends and family will suffer.

You remind me, Oh Lord, that you have a divine plan. Pain is unavoidable, but your love is unfailing. You comfort me and provide hope to me on dark days. The elimination of fear has not happened overnight. Upon beginning my faith journey, I would never have believed it possible to find myself comforted and at ease in my current life circumstances.

You are a good and gracious Lord. Your love heals and strengthens.

Amen

August 4

"For wisdom will enter your heart, and knowledge will be pleasant to your soul." Proverbs 2:10

Dear Lord,

There is so much noise and chatter in this modern world. Words, songs and soundbites get stuck in my head and play on repeat. Sometimes it becomes difficult to separate my own thoughts from those portrayed in movies, read in books or heard about in songs.

Taking quiet time out, just you and I, has become essential to discovering my truth. I pray and meditate in the morning. I go for a walk in nature. I sit quietly with my pets. After a while knowledge develops. It is a sense of wellbeing that becomes established with all that is good and right with me. The inappropriateness makes me nervous and ill at ease. In silence, you have your way of telling me how to alter course.

May I seek to make you captain of my ship, today and every day.

Amen

August 5

"If any of you lacks wisdom, you should ask God, who gives generously to all without finding fault, and it will be given to you." James 1:5

Dear Lord,

My daily devotion involves meditating on scripture and spiritual readings, as well as praying and writing. I come to you each day, pleading on my knees for you to enter any areas of my life where there are heavy burdens or cause for concern. I lay my heart and soul before you.

When I began this practice, I was desperate, but doubtful. You are filling my spirit and I continue to seek you more deeply each day. I do not have everything I wanted when I began this practice. What I have is a full and joyful life. I am attracting into my life the type of community that I crave. My life has purpose and meaning today, where initially I was a lost sheep.

You are a gracious and glorious Lord. Much gratitude I give to you today.

Amen

August 6

"'Remain in me, as I also remain in you. No branch can bear fruit by itself; it must remain in the vine. Neither can you bear fruit unless you remain in me." John 15:4

Dear Lord,

May I always be willing to seek you first in my life. I do that through my daily devotion but also in other ways. I find you in nature and I find you in quiet moments alone. I find you also in the voices of others. At times, I have found you in church however that has not always been the case.

May I be willing, Oh Lord, to always search to be in communion with you. For without that connection, I cannot grow and bear fruit. Without that connection, I have nothing to give to the world. I need to renew myself with you daily. The manner in which I discovered your presence yesterday may not be how you appear today.

Oh Lord, may I always be willing to keep an open mind in how you express yourself to me.

Amen

August 7

"'How can you say to your brother, let me take the speck out of your eye, when you fail to see the plank in your own eye?'" Luke 6:42

Dear Lord,

When I am feeling uncomfortable in myself my tendency is often to turn my focus outward. I want to look to those around me and find fault with them. For, it is always easier to see flaws in my neighbor vs. my own flaws.

Oh Lord, may I be mindful that when I am disturbed, I need to look within. I am my own greatest source of discomfort. Lord, as I move through life, it takes a lot of time and processing to adapt. Sometimes I have a tendency to become lazy. May I always accept constructive criticism and do honest self appraisals.

Amen

August 8

"Do you know your bodies are temples of the Holy Spirit, who is in you, whom you have received from God? You are not your own; you were bought at a price. Therefore honor God with your bodies." 1 Corinthians 6:19-20

Dear Lord,

In my religious practice, I feel as though my body has been quite overlooked. I have mistreated my body by being so sedentary. I have done so by eating unhealthy foods. I have done so by not showing my body and mind lovingkindness and gentle nourishment.

This has taken place over time. Please help me to be willing to seek movement meditations. I desire to make a commitment to healthy eating so that I may have more energy throughout the day with which to serve. Please help me to encourage restful sleep so that I may fully engage in your will for my life. I desire to be 100% present and alert to hear your call each day.

Amen

August 9

"'But when you pray, go into your room, close the door and pray to your Father, who is seen and unseen. Then your Father, who sees what is done in secret, will reward you.'"
Matthew 6:6

Dear Lord,

I strive to seek you each morning. I invite you in to direct my day. I structure my day around quiet time with you. My favorite time is in the morning, before the hustle and bustle of the day. The later I wait, the harder it is to devote my undivided attention.

You come to me in solitude. When I am disconnected from the noise of the world, you present yourself to me. Initially I found the quiet uncomfortable. I did not want to hear what you had to say to me as I was fearful. I savor that time now. You give me guidance and bring me peace.

Glory be to you, Oh Lord. You are my trusted friend and confidant.

Amen

August 10

"We have different gifts, according to the grace given to each of us. If your gift is prophesying, then prophesy in accordance with your faith" Romans 12:6

Dear Lord,

I am not a prophet by any stretch of the imagination. I do, however, hear you speak to me. Yesterday my husband, who I look after, was ill at ease. He was nervous and on edge. I invited him to watch TV while I slept. It was pouring rain and he was anxious. He was out of sorts and could not go for his walk.

I fell sound asleep and awoke to a dream of him roaming around confused in our neighborhood looking for me. When I awoke and looked outside, the sun was shining. I took my husband for a walk and he was soothed. Shortly thereafter, it began pouring rain again.

I am grateful for this day, Oh Lord. I am grateful for how you speak to me. Your presence in my life is real. You get messages to me when I am feeling lost and confused.

Amen

August 11

"'...From everyone who has been given much, much will be demanded; and from the one who has been entrusted with much, much more will be required." Luke 12:48

Dear Lord,

You have graciously blessed me with many gifts. In my humanness, I want to hoard these things for myself. I do not want to give financially or give of my time. There is more immediate gratification found in many distractions that present themselves in my life.

So many times, Oh Lord, I have envied a simple life. I know, however, that that is not the life you have called me to live. I know that you have called me to pour out abundant love upon your people. I can do this only as my cup runneth over from the blessings of the community about me.

Dear Lord, help me to lay my reluctance at your feet. Help me to answer your call to serve.

Amen

August 12

"Bear with each other and forgive one another if any of you has a grievance against someone. Forgive as the Lord forgave you." Colossians 3:13

Dear Lord,

Your greatest commandment for us is for us to love our neighbor. And this is such a difficult command at times, that seems so simple. We have so many different backgrounds and worldviews coming together in our society. A person who is thrust into close proximity to us may disregard some or all of our core beliefs.

May I learn to grow in understanding of those who come into my path today. May I trust that those I meet today cross my path because you want me to learn from them. The more I resist that lesson and refuse to tolerate and forgive, the more it persists.

This business of spiritual growth is difficult. May I embrace it today and every day.

Amen

August 13

"Therefore rid yourselves of all malice and all deceit, hypocrisy, envy, and slander of every kind." 1 Peter 2:1

Dear Lord,

I am not a perfect person by any stretch of the imagination. I am human, as is everyone, therefore I fall short daily of your perfection. I lay myself wholly at your feet today. I give my imperfect self to you and ask you to strengthen me so that I may endure life's daily trials.

You know me intimately, Lord. You know my fears and shortcomings. May I never preach something I do not practice. May I not judge others more harshly than I do myself. May I be mindful to extend to others the same grace that you have extended to me.

I offer myself wholly to you in my brokenness today and you strengthen me.

Amen

August 14

"So I strive to always keep my conscience clear before God and man." Acts 24:16

Dear Lord,

May I remember to regularly inventory my behavior. If I am ill at ease or if I can't sleep, may I take note of that. A regular analysis on paper is what works for me as far as exploring what weighs on my heart. This is how I identify what separates me from you. After a time of having been at this practice, I can recognize when I am off and when I need to regroup.

The right way for me to carry your message is to be fully immersed in the world. In doing so, you place me where you can use me. It is easy, however, for me to gravitate away from you, toward the shiny baubles of the world. May I always be able to carve out this time of intimacy with you; a time where I can bear my soul to you and where I can seek your comfort and guidance.

Amen

August 15

"Even though I walk through the darkest valley, I will fear no evil, for you are with me; your rod and your shaft, they comfort me." Psalm 23:4

Dear Lord,

I face many trials and challenges today, Oh Lord. You know what is on my heart. You know my struggles; health problems, addictions, pain of loss, strife in relationships, all of these can pull me into a pit of suffering. When I draw nearer to you, you bring me into genuine relation with you and with like-minded fellows. I learn that I do not need to suffer in silence.

You carry me through the darkness. You shine your light on me. May I be a beacon of light and hope to others who may be drowning under the weight of self-sufficiency. Let us all be willing to let go of pride and submit to your love. In so doing, we gain strength beyond measure; strength to endure darkness and not let our lights dim.

Amen

August 16

"The path of life leads upward for the prudent to keep them from going down to the realm of the dead." Proverbs 15:24

Dear Lord,

I seek today to follow your call to live an enlightened life. I desire to take the upper path; to keep my eyes fixed on you. Discord in relationships, illness, pain of loss, all of these can incite bitterness and pull us down into a mire of despair. May I turn my gaze upward. May I seek your guidance and your comfort.

In doing so, I allow growth. I resist stagnation. I become unstuck. It may take much work to travel the upward road. We may encounter many obstacles along the way. I recognize fellow travelers by the light in their eyes, the spring in their step and their kind words. This path is available to all who seek. As I move upward, you bring to me a like-minded community.

Amen

August 17

"Cast all your anxiety on him because he cares for you."
1 Peter 5:7

Dear Lord,

I surrender all of my worries to you. I invite your direction and care. I open my eyes to the world to see how you are working in my life to bring answers to prayers. You hear my most intimate inner dialogue. Nothing is secret from you. As I draw nearer to you each day to perform your works, it becomes clear to me that you have good things in store for me. You do have a plan for my life.

May I breathe deeply and invite calm as I remind myself that you're in charge. I do not have to do this life alone. You are my constant companion and may I always remain humble enough to remember that. I am not the one writing the script. My life has certainly not had a storybook unfolding. I may, however, get my happy ending in your kingdom nonetheless.

Amen

August 18

"Jesus looked at them and said, 'With man this is impossible, but with God all things are possible.'" Matthew 19:26

Dear Lord,

I am a lowly human. I was lost and wretched without your love and care. You have lifted me up and blessed my life abundantly. You work in me and through me to grow a genuine community about me. You blot out loneliness and isolation by providing genuine care.

It is possible for all who suffer in darkness to find their light. You have ignited a fire within me and your message burns in my heart. You have called me out of darkness to lead a full, abundant life. I endure many trials. The light of your love and the community about me make that possible. May we all learn how to walk beside one another in loving communion.

Amen

August 19

"Blessed is the one who perseveres under trial because, having stood the test, that person will receive the crown of life that God promised to those who love him." James 1:12

Dear Lord,

I have faced many struggles in my life. Currently, I bear a heavy load. There have been times that I have faltered. I have lost faith at certain times in my life and I have sought solace in the world. That way has always ultimately led to emptiness and desolation.

When I stay close to you and seek to serve you, you meet me where I am. You remove from my life those who do not belong in my current season and bring the right folks in. Your love is available, even if I fall off the beam for a time. You have allowed me to regain my close position of comfort in devotion and diligence. You are an endless source of strength. May I be a beacon of light.

Amen

August 20

"Jesus replied: 'Love the Lord your God with all your heart and with all your soul and with all your mind. This is the first and greatest commandment." Matthew 22:37

Dear Lord,

The bigger lesson I have learned throughout the course of this time has been to always put my devotion to you first. I can easily get off track. I can begin seeking the approval of others in my circle of influence. I can begin filling my mental space with media of all types. I can allow the church or the government or work to control my thoughts.

When I seek you first, above all things, everything else falls into place. I draw to myself other seekers who can walk with me on my journey. We can support each other and share learning lessons. Others who do not serve the same master lose interest over time. I feel the shift happening. I allow it today as you invite me into your presence.

Amen

August 21

"Take delight in the Lord, and he will give you the desires of your heart." Psalm 37:4

Dear Lord,

As I have learned to know you from others, I was taught to fear you. I was not capable of opening my heart fully to you. I always thought that I needed to leave my struggles and imperfections sealed up inside so that no one, especially you, could see them. What I did not realize was that you were there all the time, knowing everything; aware of my deepest, darkest secrets.

As I am learning to give myself wholly to you, I gain strength to combat my difficulties. As I open my heart to you, I allow you to love all of me. I expose my brokenness and am made whole in love. I learn to love myself and to grow closer to you each day. You do not give me everything I ask for, but you are unfolding before me a life that I never imagined.

Amen

August 22

"Wait for the Lord; be strong and take heart and wait for the Lord." Psalm 27:14

Dear Lord,

I began diligently seeking you when I was lost. I was in the wilderness in a lonely space. I was hurting and alone. I desperately wanted answers and direction in my life. I was in a desperate space.

As I draw nearer to you, I learn that this season of my life is about waiting. I can be immature and impatient, Lord. I want to grab control of the reins and write the script now. That is not, however, what you have in store for me. I have faith today that you will deliver me. What you ask from me today is devotion. As I seek you each morning, you direct my plans for the day. When I look back on several days, months, etc. I see progress.

May we all be willing to put our faith in you one day at a time.

Amen

August 23

"Devote yourselves to prayer, being watchful and thankful."
Colossians 4:2

Dear Lord,

When I am lost or floundering, I seek solace in my devotion to you. As I have journeyed through life, I have traveled through many gray areas. These are spaces where the course of action is not clear and there is a gap between natural instinct and an established teaching. In the past, I have either gone by the letter of the law, blotting out the gnawing of my inner voice, or I have so strongly followed an impulse so as to stumble.

As I mature in my faith, I learn how to diligently lay my struggles at your feet. I search your Word, I meditate, I pray over time. If I am unceasing, you illuminate my path. You make clear that I can honor my community and the indwelling within to bring a touch of your kingdom into my daily life.

Your presence today is an honor and a privilege, Lord.

Amen

August 24

"So I strive always to keep my conscience clear before God and man." Acts 24:16

Dear Lord,

I come before you daily. I examine myself regularly. I address anything that comes to the surface that does not sit right. It may take a period of time before I am willing to look at certain behaviors. There are others that are recurring character weaknesses that I regularly need to be on guard against.

I also seek to bring peace and harmony in my community. If there is something between someone else and me, I promptly seek to make it right. I am not perfect by any means. We all bump into each other as we move about and intermingle on the earth. If we strive to learn and grow in our relationships with you and with each other, however, we can become more polished over time; closer to your likeness.

Amen

August 25

"let us draw near to God with a sincere heart and with the full assurance that faith brings, having our hearts sprinkled to cleanse us from a guilty conscience and having our bodies washed with pure water." Hebrews 10:22

Dear Lord,

I seek to make contact with you each day through prayer and meditation. There are days, Lord, when I am tired. I also can get busy and allow this beautiful life to pull me away from you. When too many days go by that I am not filling myself up with you, I get off track. I begin to get a lot of feedback from the world about me.

I start letting my ego creep back in. I begin lapsing back into old behaviors. I begin getting out of alignment with your will for my life. I get further away from your kingdom. My sleep, my eating patterns and my temperament begin to become affected. There is good news, however. When I am willing to make that time and space for you again in my life, you have always entered back into relationship with me.

When I am fully connected to you, that's when I feel balanced and centered.

Amen

August 26

"But seek first his kingdom and his righteousness, and all these things will be given to you as well." Matthew 6:33

Dear Lord,

As I continue to devote myself to you, I see the life I desire unfolding before me. The unnecessary fluff falls away and I am left with all I truly need. I have genuine companionship. I have gifts to give and blessings that unfold. My anxiety dwindles as I move you more closely into the center of my world.

I still have struggles and obstacles. I have uncertainty at times regarding how to handle my issues. When I am unclear and I do not know what course to take, I can pause. I can seek you in prayer or seek advice from a trusted friend. Thank you for those gifts, Oh Lord. You have richly blessed my life.

May I be a blessing to others.

Amen

August 27

"No one can serve two masters. Either you will hate the one and love the other, or you will be devoted to one and despise the other." Matthew 6:24

Dear Lord,

You have richly blessed me and my family. I pour out my heart to you in gratitude today. As I draw nearer to you, I allow you to guide me in my career choices. We do need to earn a living, Lord. May you forgive us our transgressions when we toggle back and forth between alignment with your heavenly realm and monetary concerns.

Your calling has led me out of many jobs. Some of these jobs were quite lucrative. Please provide for me a good balance between financial security and spiritual fulfillment. Also as I am blessed, may I remember those less fortunate or those on the lower ranks trying to rise up.

Amen

August 28

"You prepare a table before me in the presence of my enemies, you anoint my head with oil and my cup overflows." Psalm 23:5

Dear Lord,

As I seek daily to walk in your ways, you bring me closer and closer into my right community. You give me the strength to withstand my critics and insulate me from the retaliation of enemies. You have richly blessed my life in more ways than I can count.

You have filled my heart and my life, Oh Lord. I have risen from poor and wretched to richly blessed. You are a good and gracious Lord, worthy of praise. You love inclusively. You avail yourself to all, not only a select few. I have my needs met today. More than that, I have pure, genuine love.

Glory and honor to you today.

Amen

August 29

"In peace I shall lie down and sleep, for you alone, Lord, make me dwell in safety." Psalm 4:8

Dear Lord,

You take care of me today. You provide for my needs. I devote myself to you and you quiet the chaos of my mind. I breathe you in and I breathe out the stress and anxiety of the world. You dwell within me and you warm my heart. You bring me into a loving community with my soul- tribe who insulate me from intruders.

There are many inner workings of my mind that I cannot share with the community. I come to you Lord, I seek solitude and solace in the safe haven that you provide. You love me despite my defects so that I may be made whole in the community of your love. Soothe my disquietude and bring me comfort today as only you can.

Amen

August 30

"Everyone ought to examine themselves before they eat of the bread and drink from the cup." I Corinthians 11:28

Dear Lord,

As I sit down to commune with you, I bring my misdeeds. I feel ill at ease; nervous about my imperfections in your sight. I allow you to see into my soul. I invite your loving and healing presence. Please guide me, direct me. As I sit, I review yesterday's activities. You illuminate me regarding where I went wrong.

May I be willing to learn; to remain teachable every day so that I may grow in your likeness. Lowly human that I am, I can never compare with your perfection. May I fill myself up with you more and more to gain strength to face my battles. May I also be able to notice behavior patterns; character flaws that make me vulnerable. May I allow you to see my vulnerability and love me back to wholeness.

Amen

August 31

"Accept one another, then, just as Christ accepted you, in order to bring praise to God." Romans 15:7

Dear Lord,

Please help me to be willing to breathe through my fear and to listen to different points of view with respect. Sometimes it is comfortable to seek out companions who are of a similar mindset. It is not healthy for me to be cloistered in sameness. Growth happens outside my comfort zone. To keep my mind active, I need to constantly challenge and expand my worldview.

May I be willing to show compassion to everyone I meet today. May I be willing to hear untraditional stories and find commonality in uncommon places. The human experience is universal. We all struggle, have joy, pain, frustration and contentment as we travel through our journey of life. May I be willing to take the hand of the outsider and welcome them into the fold.

Amen

September 1

"In their hearts humans plan their course, but the Lord establishes their steps." Proverbs 16:9

Dear Lord,

Growing up in a church as a child, I had my life all planned out. I adopted a narrative for my life and set out on a journey. As I sit here in my middle age, I am so far from the point that I set as my destination. I used to feel disappointed and disillusioned by that.

As I grow daily in faithfulness, I see that you were there all along. You carried me through so many valleys and low points so that I may get to where I am now. There is no one way of living or particular lifestyle that leads to a wholeness in you. You fill my needs in ways I could not imagine. You fortify and strengthen me to do your work.

You are a good and gracious Lord.

Amen

September 2

"One who has unreliable friends soon comes to ruin, but there is a friend who sticks closer than a brother." Proverbs 18:24

Dear Lord,

You are my closest friend and confidant. As I draw nearer and nearer to you each day, I build up a healthy community around me. I attract a genuine fellowship, united in your love. As I have gone through many friendships, I have seen many friends and associates fall away from me.

I am unexplainably blessed, Lord. When I put you first, amazing things happen. All of my false friends fall away. I had been quite lonely for some time and felt lost and barren. You are filling my life up now in just the right way. In my wildest dreams, I could not imagine who you are calling me to be. The love I have to give and receive is abundant.

Amen

September 3

"Now the Lord is the Spirit, and where the Spirit of the Lord is, there is freedom." 2 Corinthians 3:17

Dear Lord,

I invite you into my heart today and you fill me up. You bless me beyond imagination. I am free today from the bondage of the world. I do not have to live up to the expectations of the world as long as I have your love in my heart.

You call me to shine and to serve. Your spirit unites us to rise higher. We commune and transcend the confines of labels and social instincts. All are one in spirit. All can earn your freedom, I call on your name, I do your bidding and I praise your holy name.

Amen

September 4

"You have delivered me from all my troubles, and my eyes have looked in triumph on my foes." Psalm 54:7

Dear Lord,

I have had so many struggles in life. I carry a heavy burden. You do not necessarily lighten my load. You give me the strength to carry it, however. As I draw nearer to you, my character is evolving. I have an opportunity today to pursue spiritual growth as I seek you more and more each day.

I am not the same person as I was yesterday. I am a new person in the light of your love. As a result, my social circle has shifted. Many who used to look upon me with disdain have gained respect for how I live my life. Whereas I was just a taker before, I have much to give as you have richly blessed my life.

Amen

September 5

"May these words of my mouth and this meditation of my heart be pleasing in your sight, Lord, my Rock and my Redeemer." Psalm 19:14

Dear Lord,

When I was feeling lost, I began to deeply seek you through prayer and meditation. It was rough going at first. I came to you completely scared and raw. I was fearful to fully open myself to you as what had been preached to me about you was shame and judgment.

What I have found is that when I constantly show up to seek you, you meet me. You step into my life in a meaningful way. You make my broken heart whole again. May I always sing your praises and never doubt you. If I get off track or sidetracked in my practice, may I remember that you are always willing to pick me back up.

Thank you, Lord, for having a meaningful presence in my life. You avail yourself to me when I earnestly seek.

Amen.

September 6

"I know what it is to be in need, and I know what it is to have plenty. I have learned the secret of being content in any and every situation, whether well fed or hungry, whether living in plenty or in want." Philippians 4:12

Dear Lord,

You have provided for my needs. You give me a sense of wellbeing in the midst of difficulty. My struggles are many, however I am richly blessed. I am overflowing with the joy of your love. Life is difficult. You do not remove my burdens, but you help me shoulder the load.

I do not have to wander if I am lost in my troubles today. As I devote myself to you daily, you hear my pleading. I am getting direction and I am in full faith now that you have a path of deliverance for me. Each phase of life brings different obstacles. If I draw nearer to you, instead of pushing you away in anger, you help me steer the course.

Amen

September 7

"Shout for joy to the Lord, all the earth. Worship the Lord with gladness; come before him with joyful songs. Know that the Lord is God, it is he who made us, and we are his; we are his people, the sheep of his pasture." Psalm 100:1-3

Dear Lord,

I surrender my ego and selfishness. I allow you to captain my ship. When I take position under your care, my life has meaning. When I have been so down and lost, the loudest voices of the world are generally fraudulent.

When I drown out the world; when I seek quiet solitude, that is when I can hear the truth. You whisper to my soul and you fill me with the cup of your love. You lead me and guide me to return to you. You are constant and unchanging. I draw near to you and you pour out joy upon me.

Amen

September 8

"Enter his gates with thanksgiving and his courts with praise; give thanks to him and praise his name. For the Lord is good and his love endures forever." Psalm 100:4-5

Dear Lord,

I come to you in gratitude today. I feel a peace washing over me. Please help me to be alert and aware today of what is going on in my body and mind. If my intuition gives me a negative feeling about a person or a teaching, please help me to be willing to give life to that.

I am finally learning how to nurture myself spiritually. I am learning how to feel goodness and wholeness. I do not have to buy into teachings today that do not honor the being that you created me to be. You have blessed me with a strong mind and body. I draw near to you more and more each day so that you may fortify and guide me as I know you are able.

Amen

September 9

"Dear friends, let us love one another, for love comes from God. Everyone who loves has been born of God and knows God." 1 John 4:7

Dear Lord,

Let me approach all who I come in contact with today with love and compassion. You have richly blessed my life. Help me to be willing and able to pour those blessings out onto others less fortunate. There is a tendency to judge and blame the suffering for their struggles.

This is not what we who believe are called to do. Those who follow the true calling become willing to step out of their insulated world, into an authentic life experience with our less fortunate brethren. We walk alongside them and lift them up. If I am not willing to do that, and remain on the sidelines, I do not have a faith that is full and alive.

Help me to be willing to hear your call to love today.

Amen

September 10

"So whether you eat or drink or whatever you do, do it all for the glory of God." 1 Corinthians 10:31

Dear Lord,

Glory and honor to you today. I lay myself before you, I give my life to you, and you provide for my needs. I honor you with my service today and I lift up your name in my deeds. I thank you for how you have filled my cup and blessed my life.

You have given me challenges in this life, Oh Lord. You give me strength, however, to persevere. You draw others toward me who are losing faith. I minister to them in my way. I gently allow them to hurt, to grieve, to doubt and to be angry. I do for them as you do for me. I strive to give as you so generously have given to me, Oh Lord.

Amen

September 11

"Blessed is the one you discipline, Lord, the one you teach from your law" Psalm 94:12

Dear Lord,

I have shown up in my devotion to you wandering and lost. I break myself open to you on a daily basis. I was so haunted and troubled by the mess that was my life when I embarked upon this journey. I made a leap of faith and laid all of this at your feet.

You call me to a difficult task. You call me to lean into you daily. You call me into a daily surrender. Many days I show up in devotion hurried and unwilling. I do not want to rush into my day. As I force myself to pause for a period and breathe you into my soul, you richly bless the day. You fill my life abundantly.

The life I live today exceeds my wildest dreams.

Amen

September 12

"There is a time for everything, and a season for every activity under the heavens; a time to be born and a time to die, a time to plant and a time to uproot, a time to kill and a time to heal, a time to tear down and a time to build" Ecclesiastes 3:1-3

Dear Lord,

I have struggled many years in pain and darkness. I have been locked out from the sunlight of the spirit. I wandered lost and aimless in this world. I have questioned your existence and my purpose in this world.

Now as I look back I see that there was a purpose for those seasons of pain and suffering. They have made me a much more giving and compassionate person. They have strengthened me to be able to take on the challenges that I face today. When I diligently seek you, I see that there are no accidents in your kingdom.

Amen

September 13

"Each of us should please our neighbors for their good, to build them up." Romans 15:2

Dear Lord,

When I am hurt by others, when I am weary or confused, please help me to fight the urge to tear others down. Please help me to be able to retreat into my safe space, take a deep breath, and discover kindness. There are so many different people in this world from so many different backgrounds.

May I seek to edify. May I seek to look for the commonalities; to discover the humanness in all who I come into contact with. My way of processing life is no better or worse than anyone else's. Please help me to be willing to tear down old world-views that I have been subjected to that no longer serve me.

You bring exactly the right people into my life experience to instruct in your ways.

Amen

September 14

"And God is able to bless you abundantly, so that in all things, at all times, having all that you need, you will abound in every good work." 2 Corinthians 9:8

Dear Lord,

You have richly blessed my life. You provide for my needs and comfort me in times of trouble. I seek to serve you and honor you. You free me from the bondage of self and unite me in community with my fellows. As I seek to give comfort, I am thus rewarded in turn.

You provide me with a sense of genuine community and wellbeing. You invite me and others who seek you into your presence. You provide guidance and loving care. You call me into loving union with other souls. You richly bless my life.

You are a good and gracious Lord. You take care of my needs even in times of sickness and doubt.

Amen

September 15

"Therefore encourage one another and build each other up, just as in fact you are doing." 1 Thessalonians 5:11

Dear Lord,

May I seek to strengthen and edify my fellows. In turn, may I invite them to reciprocate. There have been so many squabbles and harsh words amongst your people, Lord. May we all invite lovingkindness into all communities and learn to live in loving fellowship with our diverse culture.

May we be willing to be tolerant and not reactionary. May we recognize that our ways are not the only ways. Berating and insulting are forms of abuse and should be called out when seen. All viewpoints are allowed.

May we gravitate toward our communities in lovingkindness.

Amen

September 16

"Arise, Lord! Lift up your hand, O God. Do not forget the helpless." Psalm 19:12

Dear Lord,

There is so much pain and suffering in our world today. I see so much exploitation and I am aware that what I see of what is going on only scratches the surface. There is so much oppression going on in your name. It is a source of great sadness and it has turned many against you.

You are a good and gracious Lord. You have called me out of religious oppression and given me a voice. May you do likewise in the lives of many. May we find more balance and wholeness in a world with a slanted distribution of wealth and power.

All souls are equal in your kingdom. No one is entitled to take more than their share.

Amen

September 17

"The heart of the discerning acquires knowledge, for the ears of the wise seek it out." Proverbs 18:15

Dear Lord,

I search your Word daily for guidance. I crave a message of hope in a world of darkness. Your Word breathes life into my soul, as I allow it. I find strength and patience as that is what I seek. That is my understanding of what the world needs from you now.

Whatever we seek we find in you. If we desire to overpower and oppress, we can find those messages too. I acknowledge your power and, in so doing, I am empowered. Personal power is available through your Word. We have many resources. We are not subject to the hand of any one particular person to bring a message.

The wise are capable, Oh Lord. The wise are many.

Amen

September 18

"Humble yourselves before the Lord, and he will lift you up." James 4:10

Dear Lord,

I humble myself before you today. I ask for your presence in my life to help me navigate difficult decisions. You hear my heart. You enter where others are not willing or able to go. You provide guidance and direction in troubled times.

There have been many times in my life where I have been standing at a crossroads. I am very blessed today to have you as my companion. As I draw near, as I ask for you to enter in, you do. You whisper to me the next right action to take. I do not see the whole picture. You reveal your will to me one step at a time. Today you show me to walk through pain, let go of worldly attachments, and trust you for a good outcome.

Today I choose to comply.

Amen

September 19

"Pay attention and turn your ear to the sayings of the wise; apply your heart to what I teach" Proverbs 22:17

Dear Lord,

There are so many personalities out there with so many different opinions. Different teachers have different plans to follow for a happy and fulfilling life. My life story has never been one to fit neatly in the box. I have seen so many disillusioned by following blindly.

As I deepen my practice, I draw nearer to you each day. I become united in community with others who seek your wisdom in kind. We fortify and strengthen one another. We instruct and correct. I study your Word, and the inspired Words of many as I seek to fulfill my purpose in this life. I listen, read, diligently pray, meditate, ask questions and follow my intuition. I pause when uncertain and repent when I transgress.

I surrender and trust you to chart my course.

Amen

September 20

"Cast your cares on the Lord and he will sustain you; he will never let the righteous be shaken." Psalm 55:22

Dear Lord,

I offer my burdens to you today. I surrender my cares and concerns. You hear my desperate pleas and you fortify and strengthen me. You have everything all worked out for me. I do not need to worry about the ultimate plan for my life. I need to show up each morning, diligently seek your presence and guidance and take one step at a time.

Over time, you will reveal your design for my life. I need to do the footwork during the day and surrender my cares to you at night. Then I need to get up and do the whole process over again. As I have been doing this over a period of time, you have blessed me abundantly in previously unimaginable ways.

Please help me, Oh Lord, to be willing to follow you to the end of my days.

Amen

September 21

"'Why do you look at the speck of sawdust in your brother's eye and pay no attention to the plank in your own eye?'" Matthew 7:3

Dear Lord,

I will never follow all of your commands fully. I will err time and time again in my human way. May I not look with scorn on others as I gain awareness of their imperfections. May I practice patience and tolerance so that I may receive that in turn.

I should focus my attention on myself. I should regularly examine my own behavior and work to remove my shortcomings. I invite you into my humanness today, Oh Lord. I give myself wholly to you so that you may have all of me. I am simply your humble servant.

Call me where I am needed, Oh Lord.

Amen

September 22

"Dear children, let us not love with words or speech but with actions and in truth." 1 John 4:18

Dear Lord,

It is easy to preach a message of love, When it comes right down to the active practice of loving those who struggle with the disease of addiction, it is more difficult. When it comes down to me loving those with differing beliefs, or those who are resentful of me, it is a lot more difficult.

It can begin with a warm look, or just a slight smile. Sometimes a simple acknowledgement is a firm beginning. Some will hear me and some will not. Some will only see my actions and behavior and understand. In the end, love is a feeling. If I preach love but do not radiate that I will be known to preach a false doctrine.

Lord, may I be a vessel, an instrument of the love you have given me.

Amen

September 23

"Let us therefore make every effort to do what leads to peace and to mutual edification." Romans 14:19

Dear Lord,

There is so much discord in your world. There is so much fighting and people have been divided into so many different camps. May we all work to lay aside our egos today. May we lay down our swords and soften to hear each other.

We may not find understanding or a warm embrace initially. We may find a compromise. May we find tolerance. As I tolerate, I grow in my own understanding. I think that this would be the case for all. May we seek to reward, not to oppress. May we not hoard but may we share graciously with one another.

The larger our family of friends the greater our reward in heaven, Oh Lord.

Amen

September 24

"Take delight in the Lord, and he will give you the desires of your heart" Psalm 37:4

Dear Lord,

I fill my heart with a message of truth and love. It is a day that belongs to you and I lean into my devotion today. I connect myself to a like-minded community and hear how other folks are experiencing you today. You are alive in my life today.

Your message evolves and makes itself true in changing times. A new community embraces me and I am molded, shaped and adapted for the next phase of my life. You are universal. You have been with us throughout time. You avail yourself in many ways. Your truth is comprehensible in each of our lives, should we choose to seek it.

You fulfill my dreams as I work to know you. When I learn to trust you, you reveal yourself.

Amen

September 25

"In all my prayers for all of you, I always pray with joy…"
Philippians 1:4

Dear Lord,

I pray for our world. I pray for all people. We are in so much disagreement. We are warring with each other. We try to outdo each other. But I see the goodness and I pray for the best in all people. I see beautiful cultures, amazing foods, glorious arts, and wonderful voices with many stories to tell.

I pray, Oh Lord, with joy and appreciation for the beautiful humanness that unites us. We are all joined in craving a sense of belonging in this world. I am humbled by my origin story. I am an underdog. I hail from impoverished immigrants. I am neurotic and noticeably flawed. Yet I have found joy in my life, in my middle-class culture.

I pray the same for all people. I pray that all people may find joy in themselves and I maintain hope for humanity.

Amen

September 26

"May the God who gives endurance and encouragement give you the same attitude of mind toward each other that Christ Jesus had" Romans 15:15

Dear Lord,

I diligently pray to you each day. I pour out my heart to you. You have become my constant companion. In my family, we have many afflictions. We have tough days. We have painful days, both physically and emotionally. Sometimes it feels as though we will crack under the pressure. We endure, however, our faith prevails.

I am hopeful about your promises of deliverance. You send your messages to me when I am at my breaking point to let me know that I am not alone. You are good to me. You meet me where I am when I call out your name. You do not give me more than I can handle and you strengthen me in ways I could not imagine.

Amen

September 27

""But if we walk in the light, we have fellowship with one another.."1 John 1:7

Dear Lord,

Your presence is mighty and you have gifted me with many great fellows. I do not need to come to a church building to sit in your presence. I can come together with brothers and sisters in your name and commune with the divine. If we earnestly seek together, there shall be a light.

May I bring your glory and your rays of joy to darkened souls. We think we find joy in action; in the busyness. The joy is in the moment, when we can sit still and breathe your light into the darkened recesses of the soul. It's when we can commune, not with words but with a look, a touch, a general knowing to connect with humanity.

Lord please help me to seek fewer words today. Please help me to tune in and to just be with others in a combined presence.

Amen

September 28

"Gather to me this consecrated people, who made a covenant with me by sacrifice." Psalm 50:5

Dear Lord,

I take your yoke upon me as I choose to seek you each day. You recognize all who work to try to hear your voice. You honor me. You provide me with a holy union with my fellows. We show up for each other. We become willing to have a real and true presence in each other's lives.

What do I sacrifice? I sacrifice my ego. I sacrifice my selfishness. I humble myself before you and allow you to take the wheel. I am not in charge. Only you know the best course. Only you know what is best for me. No one person can step into this authoritarian role in my life. Only you are sovereign.

I turn my power over to you today. I allow you to guide and direct me.

Amen

September 29

"Praise be to the Lord God, the God of Israel, who alone has marvelous deeds" Psalm 72:18

Dear Lord,

I sing your praises today. You are good, you are gracious, you are kind, you are patient, you are gentle. I seek to mirror these qualities. You can also be stern and you discipline me when I am needing structure. I no longer fear this when it comes as I am always better for it in the end.

Through you I have been triumphant over addiction. You have calmed me when I was anxious and you have provided community in times of despair. You have warmed my heart in times of fear and struggle. You cloak me in your love so that I may serve the sick and advocate for the marginalized.

Use me Oh Lord. May I serve a great purpose in your kingdom.

Amen

September 30

"May your unfailing love be my comfort, according to your promise to your servant." Psalm 119:76

Dear Lord,

I have many struggles. Sometimes there is pain. You do not take that away. I must be human and live in this crazy, beautiful world you have given us. You allow me to lay my head on your shoulder and feel. You provide comfort and safety where I don't have to fear my feelings or run from them.

You also provide for my fellows who walk with me through the pain. The burdens are not removed, but I become fortified and encouraged. As time marches on and I continue on my journey, there are many goodbyes to be said. It hurts my heart but you allow me space and time to process and heal. As I empty myself to you, you bring me to the next phase of lighted love.

Your love exceeds my expectations, Oh Lord.

Amen

October 1

"And he who searches our hearts knows the mind of the Spirit, because the spirit intercedes for God's people in accordance with the will of God." Romans 8:27

Dear Lord,

You only know my truest self. I am many people. Sometimes I feel lost in my many roles. As I commune with you each day I invite in the light of your truth. No words are needed; simply silent communion.

I summon your spirit; awaken within me and burn my heart to do your will. Help me to be your messenger. Help me to remember to care for my own needs also. I cannot serve with any type of endurance if I am not practicing self-care.

Take all of me, Lord. Strengthen me where I am weak. Help me to use my talents to best serve.

Amen

October 2

"You became imitators of us and of the Lord, for you welcomed the message in the midst of severe suffering with the joy given by the Holy Spirit." 1 Thessalonians 1:6

Dear Lord,

May I continue to seek daily how to walk in your ways. As I lean in deeper and deeper a community builds up around me that is so glorious and edifying. In my immense pain, I can carry joy in my heart and bring that to others who struggle.

I have made you my close friend and confidant. I diligently search your Word. I connect with and share ideas among other like-minded people. We fortify each other and build each other up. You show me how to nurture myself and my faith. Each day, the next right step along the journey is a lot clearer.

I rely on you with assurance and you do not lead me astray.

Amen

October 3

"The Spirit of God has made me, the breath of the Almighty gives me life." Job 33:4

Dear Lord,

I praise you with gratitude today. You fill the empty holes in my life and my spirit a bit more each day. You have not blessed me with the perfect family or the best home on the block. But my life is rich and full today in ways that it was not one year ago.

You fill my lungs with cleansing breath and I am grounded. I have resources when I start to get carried away by the cares of the world. You keep me safe, you teach me how to feed myself, how to provide love and care and how to get my needs met.

Glory and honor be to you today, Oh Lord.

Amen

October 4

"Give careful thought to the path for your feet and be steadfast in all your ways." Proverbs 4:26

Dear Lord,

I come to you today to seek guidance. I lay my questions at your feet and seek direction. I have not always been so careful with my decision making. I have gotten myself into some tough spots. I have stumbled before and will stumble again in some way.

May I continually seek to grow in your ways. Will you please give me patience and strength as that is the path I need to follow today. Many things can pull me off course or cause me to feel self-pity. You bring me into contact with others, however. I hear your voice speak through them when I am in the wilderness.

Bless this day as you meet me where I am. You light my way in the darkness when I seek you.

Amen

October 5

"If an enemy were insulting me, I could endure it; if a foe were rising against me, I could hide." Psalm 55:12

Dear Lord,

Not all who encounter me embrace me in kindness. Some find my ways and understandings quite unorthodox. I have forced myself into many roles that did not suit me. When I broke free there was chaos and discord. I hold no resentment, however, I am grateful.

I have gleaned from each role a small part of who I am. I am a mature woman and I am content with myself. I am not damaged or unholy. I am uniquely myself, made perfect in your love. I invite the outcasts into fellowship and we embrace each other in wholeness.

There is a place for all in this world. May we believe and embrace community.

Amen

October 6

"Live in harmony with one another. Do not be proud, but be willing to associate with people of low position. Do not be conceited." Romans 12:16

Dear Lord,

Please help me to ground myself in humility today. May I seek to be generous and of service rather than placing myself on a higher plane. Help me to always remember my roots and how I was when I had shut you out of my life.

I was an outcast. I was lost and downtrodden. You have brought me into holy communion with your grace. May I witness that to other seekers, not condemn them. I know you have called me out, not so I can turn my back on my past, but so that I may look back to lift others up.

Amen

October 7

"He changes times and seasons; he deposes kings and raises up others. He gives wisdom to the wise and knowledge to the discerning." Daniel 2:21

Dear Lord,

It seems times are so troubled right now. We do not have good leadership in our world. We do not have reliable sources of information at our fingertips. As we study history or look through the scriptures, we learn that these struggles are not unique to the present time period.

The world is fickle. Only your love is unchanging. You shine the light of truth in the lives of the seekers. You provide enlightenment in times of confusion. You breathe calm into my heart and invite peace into my soul. Please direct me today in how to conduct myself in my personal relationships.

Amen

October 8

"For where you have envy and selfish ambition, there you find disorder and every evil practice." James 3:16

Dear Lord,

I have lived another life. I have been so negative, angry and resentful. I have been paralyzed by fear and hatred. I drew to myself other fellows who lived in that same space. We were hurt. We were traumatized. We hurt and traumatized each other and pushed goodness further from our lives.

This is how disease and disorder breeds. As I move more into another space, things are beginning to shift. As I seek wellness, as I seek healing, I step into a new world. I make a leap of faith and attempt to believe that your presence is available to me in my brokenness. I believe that maybe I can be restored to wholeness. As I continue to do this unwaveringly, it is slowly happening.

Amen

October 9

"The one who gets wisdom loves life; the one who cherishes understanding will soon prosper." Proverbs 19:8

Dear Lord,

I pray for wisdom in my life and in my choices today. I seek you in all things, dear Lord. Sometimes the path is clear and sometimes it is not. I continue diligently to seek nonetheless. I have others in my life who similarly seek. I can take the advice of wise counsel as well if I am at a crossroads.

As I have chosen this path, you have blessed my life abundantly. I continue to seek as new and developing challenges present themselves. So many are suffering or dying at this time. I have many of my own struggles. You provide the community that I need in order to get through the challenges.

Amen

October 10

"'I have told you these things, so that in me you will have peace. In this world you will have trouble. But take heart! I have overcome the world." John 16:33

Dear Lord,

I carry a great number of difficulties. There are days that I feel as though I want to run and hide away. The only way out is through, as my community of believers has taught me. I, therefore, lay my cares at your feet each day. I give you my sorrow. I give you my heartache.

There is the pain of loss. There is fear of the unknown. I invite you into that space, Oh Lord. I feel the indwelling and become strengthened. No one is spared the heartache of the world. The joy comes from the shared community of those who also invite the joy of your love into their lives.

I thank you today, Oh Lord, for another day.

Amen

October 11

"You have set our inequities before you, our secret sins in the light of your presence." Psalm 90:8

Dear Lord,

I am an imperfect human. I pour out my heart to you today; I give you the good and the bad that make up my character. I ask that you will allow me to grow closer to you. I ask that you will mold me more into your likeness.

We are all perfect in our brokenness. We are all made whole in our union with you. May you search my heart today and know my shortcomings. May I seek to be of service to others and not to fester in my selfish negativity. Self-righteousness is an easy path. Self-examination is the more godly way. May I remain willing to strengthen my spirit in your love.

Amen

October 12

"After he had dismissed them, he went up on a mountainside by himself to pray. Later that night, he was there alone" Matthew 14:23

Dear Lord,

May I remember to imitate your example when I am facing trials and am not knowing which way to turn. May I seek you alone. May I continue to carve out quiet time with you where I may hear your voice speak to me. There are a lot of things vying for my attention.

When I am burdened with decisions, I have made it my practice to seek you. I pause and I pray and I ask for your direction and care. If I am uncertain, I wait. Please help me to continue to do this with you regarding big decisions or when I am at a crossroads.

Please strengthen me and guide me as only you can.

Amen

October 13

"And do not forget to do good and to share with others. For with such sacrifices, God is well pleased." Hebrews 13:16

Dear Lord,

May I be generous. May I not forget to distribute a portion of my time and my blessings with those less fortunate. Please help all those who have been blessed to remember to lend a hand to those who are struggling. In so doing, the givers receive your grace.

May I be willing to hear your call; to know the best use of my resources. Each one of us has many gifts that can be shared. As we give and take amongst ourselves, we build a community. May I not close my eyes to those struggling around me. Right in our backyard there are those who are hurting.

May I always seek to give abundantly, Oh Lord.

Amen

October 14

"Lord, you establish peace for us; all that we have accomplished you have done for us." Isaiah 26:12

Dear Lord,

You have carried me away from brokenness. You have given me a new life in service to you. You have blessed me abundantly. I was once downtrodden and you have lifted me up. My struggles continue to be many, however you take the burden from me and strengthen me in your love.

You have taken the stress and anxiety from my shoulders. You provide peace and comfort. All I need to do is surrender my cares to you each day. I need to remain mindful that I cannot do life on my own. I need to be in constant remembrance of the need for your presence in my life.

You have taken my troubles, Oh Lord, and replaced them with blessings.

Amen

October 15

"But the plans of the Lord stand firm forever, the purposes of his heart through all generations." Psalm 33:11

Dear Lord,

You have called me to a purpose. I have a place in this life and I have a duty to perform. You have placed many people in my life who are wanting love. It is my privilege to love them. In return, I receive love.

You have called many throughout time. You give large portions to those who are called into your grace. The culture needs to change over time. The sentiment of giving evolves and the need does not remain constant either. May we always be willing to hear different voices. May we be willing to speak up about our various journeys.

Amen

October 16

"Rather, it should be that of your inner self, the unfading beauty of a gentle and quiet spirit, which is of great worth in God's sight." 1 Peter 2:4

Dear Lord,

May I seek you today as I quiet my mind and allow my soul to rest in you. May I focus my attention on my own affairs, and not meddle in the business of others. May I be a model of love and service. May I bring light to those suffering in darkness.

May I use my gifts to edify and lift you up in goodness. May I put down distraction and seek wholeness. May I be careful with my words. May I not indulge in idle chatter and may I choose my words appropriately. May my language be appropriate to my audience.

Amen

October 17

"I have no one else like him, who will show genuine concern for your welfare." Philippians 2:20

Dear Lord,

May we be as disciples unto your name. May we walk in your footsteps and emulate your ways. May we think genuinely of the welfare of others and make that our life's mission. When we are blessed enough to be called out of lowly beginnings, may we always be willing to reach back down to those who remain in bondage.

As we have been helped, may we help others. Let us not allow the goodness of your name to be forgotten. May we bear witness to the greatness of your love not boast of our knowledge of your laws. Coldheartedness and condemnation will only push a seeker further away.

Thank you, Oh Lord, for sending these great examples. Let us learn from them, Oh Lord.

Amen

October 18

"For it is by grace you have been saved, through faith – and this is not from yourselves, it is the gift of God – not by works, so that no one can boast." Ephesians 2:8-9

Dear Lord,

Your love is a blessing I have not earned or deserved. Your grace has blessed me and from that place of gratitude I serve. I am not saved through the works that I perform. Please continue to bless me so that I am filled up. Let me in turn bless others.

You have called me out of pain and chaos, Oh Lord. You have brought me into a loving community. May that perfect love remain available to all to freely step into. May I work to give back what has been so freely given to me.

Amen

October 19

"'My prayer is not for them alone. I pray also for those who will believe in me through their message'" John 17:20

Dear Lord,

May I be your true disciple. May I carry your message not so much in word but in deed. For I have responded to your call primarily as a result of the love that has been shown to me. I have not responded because I have been preached to or condemned. Your message is carried in love and inclusion.

Love lives in action. Love lives in walking into a meaningful life experience with those that are hurting. Most often they will not seek refuge in a church. The message needs to be carried into their reality. Generally, in the church there is a uniformity. I seek the different; the unique. I look for the hurting. I look for a disconnect. I look for pain.

Love binds. Love heals. Love forgives.

Amen

October 20

"Fools show their annoyance at once, but the prudent overlook an insult." Proverbs 12:16

Dear Lord,

When I am out in the world, interacting, I come up against a lot of feedback. When I meet people who are different from me, racially, culturally, generationally, I come up against a lot of criticism. There are a lot of assumptions and a lot of people are distrusting of things and people who are different from them.

May I be prudent today in these situations. May I allow first impressions. May I give all an opportunity to experience me as an individual and help form me into a more fully evolved human being. May we journey together on a path that is closer to your likeness, messy as that may be.

May I not be foolish in my interactions today, Oh Lord.

Amen

October 21

"He must manage his own family well and see that his children obey him, and he must do so in a manner worthy of full respect." 1 Timothy 3:4

Dear Lord,

I involve myself in so many endeavors. Sometimes I spread myself too thin. May I be attentive today in all I do. May I scale back on my involvements, if I am not putting my whole heart and soul into them. If I seek to be too self-serving in how I spend my time, may I be willing to alter my course.

My focus today is family. It is on caring for the youth and the underserved. It is carrying a hopeful message of your love beyond measure that is available to all. It is in being broken open regarding the pain of human existence. It is about the healing power of your love and the community it brings.

If something I do does not serve these purposes, help me to be able to recognize that.

Amen

October 22

"In the shelter of your presence you hide from them for all human intrigues; you keep them safe in your dwelling from accusing tongues." Psalm 31:20

Dear Lord,

I hear much criticism, day in and day out. Although it may sting initially I do not take that to heart. I use that to become a more fully evolved person. I know that you love me as I am. In my imperfect human form. You meet me where I am and invite me to grow in the comfort of your presence.

This shelter is available to all. It is the comfort of a home inside the soul that invites us to recharge after days on the battlefield of life. As long as we live, we will be confronted with the pain of our shortcomings on a daily basis. Your love offers the healing power of spiritual growth, your generous gift.

Please help me to soften to the growth process, Lord.

Amen

October 23

"But let all who take refuge in you be glad; let them ever sing for joy. Spread your protection over them, that those who love your name may rejoice in you." Psalm 5:11

Dear Lord,

You have provided for my needs. You provide shelter and safety. You give me a refuge to retreat to after the difficulties of my day. You do not spare me from trouble. You do not take away all of my difficulties. You do give me comfort and warmth to nurture my soul so that I may go back out onto the battlefield.

All your praise I give to you. May the world see love as witnessed through me. May those who are suffering find a way out through the light of your love as I have. May there be others who are willing to give of themselves to help shine a light into their experience.

Amen

October 24

"Turn your ear to me, come quickly to my rescue; be my rock of refuge, a strong fortress to save me." Psalm 31:2

Dear Lord,

Hear my cry as I come to you in uncertainty. I lay my troubles at your feet and request your presence. I ask that you listen to my heart as only you know what I need. When I sit with you, the fog lifts. I do not feel so confused. I feel at peace with not knowing.

I am blessed today in that I can seek your council, I can wait for clear direction. I can trust my instincts and if something does not seem right, I can pause. I can request that you provide clarity. This is a gift that comes as we spiritually mature, I am finding that I do not have to solve all of the world's problems today.

Just for today, may I do the work that you present to me. May I surrender to the outcome and to your care.

Amen

October 25

"Therefore you do not lack any spiritual gift as you eagerly wait for our Lord Jesus Christ to be revealed." 1 Corinthians 1:7

Dear Lord,

As we move through life, it is easy to get caught up in comparing our lives to the lives of others. It is easy to look at our neighbors' lives and see everything they have or appear to have and to want those things for ourselves. What I need to constantly remind myself of is that I have been made exactly as I should be, with all of the gifts you intended for me.

I need to remember that we are all flowing with abundance. We all have gifts that can be harnessed according to your calling. There is goodness, Lord. There is divine order and harmony if we seek those things. They may not come together as a united whole in the brokenness of our lives. Only in community do we complete each other.

Amen

October 26

"But he said to me, 'My grace is sufficient for you, for my power is perfect in weakness.' Therefore I will boast all the more gladly about my weaknesses, so that Christ's power may rest on me." 2 Corinthians 12:9

Dear Lord,

I come before you today as an imperfect person. I carry with me mental constructs passed down to me by my ancestors who labored and struggled through this life. May I allow my world-view to stretch beyond its present capacity. May I remain teachable and may I soften to new ideas and new understandings, even in my old age.

I am weak in my limited worldview. Please help me to be willing to extend myself where needed and to not be fearful of those who do not present to me in a way that is familiar. Please bring to me those who seek to learn from me and also those who I can learn from. Help me to bring comfort where there is discord, dear Lord.

Amen

October 27

"for it is God who works in you to will and to act in order to fulfill his good purpose." Philippians 2:13

Dear Lord,

Please use me today as an instrument of your ways. Please help me to remove ego from my thoughts and actions. Please help me to practice loving tolerance. My human instinct is to want to have ideas and to be given credit for those ideas.

The truth is that it is nothing of myself that brings goodness and wholeness. Anything to do with self only divides. It does not heal. When I seek your higher calling, I can allow you to work in and through me. I see goodness in this world. I see diversity. I see a colorful world. I hear a message that needs to be shared. May we speak it in an edifying manner. May we allow a collective benevolence as we consult you each day in how to live.

Amen

October 28

"Trust in him at all times, you people; pour out your hearts to him, for God is our refuge." Psalm 62:8

Dear Lord,

Only you are there for me unconditionally. You have been my constant companion throughout my life. You have brought me out of darkness and you have given me many blessings. When I struggle, I take comfort in you. You hear my pleas for help and you bring help. It may not come in my time, but yet it comes.

You are my confidant and the foundation upon which my life is built. Everything springs forth from the love you have given unto me. As you have blessed me and as you nurse my wounded soul back to health, I sing your praises. I owe my life to you. You have richly blessed my life.

Amen

October 29

"A false witness will perish, but a careful listener will testify successfully." 21:28

Dear Lord,

I speak of nothing I do not have experience with. I have followed in your ways, I have faltered, I have fallen and I have gotten back up. I seek, I waiver, I get off course at times and yet, I continue seeking. You are my driving force. I let your spirit work in and through me.

You have placed me where you need me. You call me each day to dig in deeper in carrying your message. As I grow in your love, my community builds and thrives. I am not alone. Many walk the path of love along with me. As false profits gradually fall away, very few remain standing.

Amen

October 30

"Test me, Lord, and try me, examine my heart and my mind" Psalm 26:2

Dear Lord,

I humble myself before you. I leave behind the quick fixes and the false promises of the world. I lay down my defenses and earnestly seek the truth. The world I am living in is changing and I ask for perseverance and presence of mind to be able to let go of old world-views and adapt.

May I be able to let go of outdated concepts and embrace renewal. May I be able to find a place for me and my clan in the revolution as it unfolds. My belief in you needs to be fluid. I cannot understand faith in the way that I used to as there were many flaws and limitations in the fabric of those understandings.

Forgive me my prior shortcomings. Help me to welcome diversity and my place therein.

Amen

October 31

"'I have much more to say to you, more than you can now bear. But when he, the Spirit of truth, comes, he will guide you into all truth. He will not speak on his own; he will speak only what he hears, and he will tell you what is yet to come.'" John 16:12-13

Dear Lord,

I seek you each day in prayer and devotion. When we empty ourselves to you, there is an indwelling Spirit, a piece of you that resides in us. May I be able to tap into that source for guidance, direction and strength.

When I allow it, you avail yourself to me in this way. Yes, there are times when I can't get out of my own way. There are times when I want something so badly that it is hard to see that your will is something other than what I desire. May I fully surrender to you today. May I humbly take my place in your kingdom.

Amen

November 1

"'Give, and it will be given to you. A good measure, pressed down, shaken together and running over, will be poured into your lap. For with the measure you use, it will be measured to you'" Luke 6:38

Dear Lord,

As I give of myself and of my means, you return rewards back to me abundantly. Sometimes we may feel as though we have been slighted and we want to hoard our blessings. May I always remember your loving guidance. May I be willing to give, knowing that I will be blessed in return.

No man is an island. We are all interrelated. When one suffers, we all suffer. If others suffer from lack, how can I continue to build an empire in greed? Please direct me as to where there is the greatest need, to know how I can make the largest contribution.

Amen

November 2

"They want to be teachers of the law, but they do not know what they are talking about or what they so confidently affirm." 1 Timothy 1:7

Dear Lord,

I have seen much corruption and confusion in the modern institution of the church. May we remember, Lord, that we are all equal in your love. No one can invalidate our experience of truth in our lives. I am free to seek you in my own time and in my own way.

May no one feel the need to conform to toxic or abusive expressions of faith. May we find you in our own way. May we create our own silent devotion. May we build our own community. May we seek to love and be loved as your commands call us to do.

Your love is good, honest and pure. It is not oppressive.

Amen

November 3

"The lips of the righteous nourish many, but fools die for lack of sense." Proverbs 10:21

Dear Lord,

May I seek to always edify and lift others up, not to bring them down. May I study and educate myself before speaking. It is so easy to lash out verbally when we are feeling deeply. It is often a reflex response to try to hurt others when we have been hurt ourselves.

Today may I own my own pain. May I dive deeply into your healing power and seek solution-oriented discussion. If none can be found immediately, may I walk away and decompress for a while. So many of us with personal and cultural differences are collaborating and challenging growth within one another.

May I not resist this growth. May I speak only of your healing love and care.

Amen

November 4

"'Forgive us our sins, for we also forgive everyone who sins against us. And lead us not into temptation.'" Luke 11:4

Dear Lord,

I come before you as a human with many shortcomings. Please help me to be awake and aware of any harm I may do. May I seek to soften and forgive harms done to me. May I be alert to that which may pull me off course today.

Each one of us is hard-wired for imperfection. May we know and study ourselves. May we strengthen ourselves through prayer and devotion so that we cause minimal harm in our inevitable transgressions. May we come together to fortify each other; to admit our defects and move toward more godly ways.

Please embrace me in my brokenness. May I, in turn, embrace the whole of humankind.

Amen

November 5

"You have made known to me the path of life; you will fill me with joy in your presence." Acts 2:28

Dear Lord,

I seek you each day in prayer and meditation. I humble myself before you to ask you to remove my ego and fill me with your Spirit. I come to you when I am feeling lost and I ask you to direct me. I do not always know where I am going, but you tell me the next right action to take.

As I do this over a period of time you prove to me that you do have a design for my life. You give me confidence and joy in your love. You provide for me even when I doubt you or am low on faith. I no longer doubt you. I see more clearly where you are calling me.

May I always be willing to hear your still, small voice.

Amen

November 6

"It is true that some preach Christ out of envy and rivalry, but others out of goodwill." Philippians 1:15

Dear Lord,

Please help me to be mindful of your instructions as you reveal yourself to me today. Please help me to seek solitude and quiet reflection. I want to pursue a relationship with you. May I take pride in the day's work and not compare myself to others.

May I allow others their inner space today. May I focus my efforts on cleaning up my side of the street, not on chasing what others have with envy. When I focus on making myself grow in your ways, I attract positive attention to myself and glorify you.

Amen

November 7

"Hear my cry for help, my king and my God, for to you I pray." Psalm 5:2

Dear Lord,

At times the weight of this life is heavy on my shoulders. I can get to where I feel as though I am going to break. Instead of giving up or throwing in the towel, I turn to you. I give to you my family, my health problems, my addictions. I give it all to you today, Oh Lord.

I ask for your protection and care. I pray that you strengthen me to carry the burdens that I face on a daily basis. I ask and I ask and I don't stop asking. I am relentless in my pursuit of you. I chase you with faith and with perseverance. In time, you do deliver me. You provide a community surrounding me that is willing and able to walk with me and to fortify me.

Great is your love, Oh Lord.

Amen

November 8

"In the morning, Lord, you hear my voice; in the morning I lay my requests before you and wait expectantly." Psalm 5:3

Dear Lord,

I greet you in the morning. I open my heart up to you. I come to you and ask for your direction and care. I lay my burdens at your feet and you lift me up when I am confused or in doubt. When I do not hear you speak clearly to me, I wait on you.

Waiting can be difficult. It is difficult to be in a time of unknowing. Somehow I feel as though I have to explain everything or write a script. Most of the time, I have to throw up my hands and give things over to you. I surrender to you today. I give you my incomplete, imperfect self and ask that you form me more closely into your likeness.

Today I will be patient and wait for further instruction.

Amen

November 9

"these are the things God has revealed to us by his Spirit. The Spirit searches all things, even the deep things of God." 1 Corinthians 2:10

Dear Lord,

May I love and honor all of humankind. May I distance myself from those engaging in toxic behavioral expressions, but may I love them from afar. May I not turn a blind eye to human suffering. I also have my own suffering and your love has blessed me with like-minded folks who are willing to step into my pain and help carry my load.

May we all be willing to commune with one another in that regard. There is a time and a place for pretense, however, among our intimate associates may we leave that behind. Let us not snap into judgment when observing the behavior of others. May we soften our hearts and hold our tongues.

Amen

November 10

"Finally, all of you, be like-minded, be sympathetic, love one another, be compassionate and humble." 1 Peter 3:8

Dear Lord,

Please help me to choose my intimate circle wisely. Please help me to reach my hand up for my associates so as not to elevate myself. Help me to learn to let go of my toxic ways. Help me also to be willing to continue working on myself so that I will not be considered a person of bad character.

As I learn to let go of my old behavior, may I go in search of those wanting to break free. May I be able to keep a healthy detachment so as not to be brought back down. May I never stop reaching down, however, to lift up those below and wanting to break free. I am where I am today only because there were people that refused to give up on me.

You never gave up on me. For this I sing your praises.

Amen

November 11

"They will still bear fruit in their old age, they will stay fresh and green" Psalm 92:14

Dear Lord,

I am not a young woman. May I never stop being teachable, however, may I allow the young people to open my eyes to their life experiences. May I be willing to hear other voices, other stories. May I honor a variety of experiences of truth. There is no one path to enlightenment. Although I may choose you and your words as my avenue, there are other viable paths to the truth.

May I give credibility today to diversity. May I shun homogeneous environments. May I experience the validity of the human experience. I have spent so much of my life trying to fit the mold. The youth are teaching me. I can allow my individuality. I can allow myself to think creatively and independently.

You have blessed me with these gifts, Lord, may I use them.

Amen

November 12

"His divine power has given us everything we need for a godly life through our knowledge of him who called us by his own glory and goodness." 2 Peter 1:3

Dear Lord,

As I have come to diligently seek you, you reveal yourself to me. Your ways and your power are available to all who pursue you in this way. Your words inspire me today. May they reach others in this way, as is your intent.

I pour out my heart to you and let you breathe life back into me. You help me to interpret your message as it is intended for my own understanding. May you call others to respond in kind as you have richly blessed my life and your blessings abound. You listen and provide your comfort and care.

Great are your provisions, Oh Lord. May I always make you my primary focus.

Amen

November 13

"For everything God created is good, and nothing is to be rejected if it is received with thanksgiving, because it is constantly by word of God and prayer." 1 Timothy 4:4

Dear Lord,

I offer up my gratitude to you today. You have surrounded me with family and friends. You provide a community that honors my individuality. You do not force me to be anything that I am not capable of being. You challenge me. You push me to my limits.

Just when I feel I am going to break, I cry out and you come to me. You speak to me as a still, small voice inside of me. When I am so out of touch that I am unable to hear you, you speak to me through others. Even when I deliberately shut you out, you pursue me.

For this, I am grateful, I have learned to trust you and you richly bless me. May others be willing to open up to you in this way.

Amen

November 14

"Though an army beseige me, my heart will not fear; though war break out against me, even then I will be confident." Psalm 27:3

Dear Lord,

May I be willing to step into your offering. I was raised with teachings of you waiting to punish me and that has incited fear. Instead, I am coming to understand you as a tender being who wants to gently invite me into a loving partnership with you.

The punishment is something that I do to myself when I deliberately pull away from you. It does not feel safe and secure for me when I do this. In my mind it can seem as though this is something you are doing for me when, I instead begin to move closer. When I allow your love, the fear dissipates.

May I always maintain a willingness to draw closer, instead of retreating in tough times.

Amen

November 15

"for God's gifts and his call are irrevocable." Romans 11:29

Dear Lord,

You have richly blessed my life. You move me to give back in turn. I only have what I have as I received your message from some who refused to give up on me when I had fallen on hard times. Please show me how to best return that gift.

For many years I have been reluctant to step into this role of responsibility. It is easy to become lazy and resentful and for me to feel as though I just want to look after myself. This is not what you have called me to do. You have called me to a mission. May I never shirk my responsibilities.

Amen

November 16

"Hold them in the highest regard in love because of their work. Live in peace with each other." 1 Thessalonians 5:13

Dear Lord,

Your message is one of hope and strength. It is available to all regardless of status or background. No one person is more receptive than another. May I continue to diversify my life experiences so that I may speak meaningfully of your ways to many.

I do not elevate myself as a leader. I take no credit for how richly you have blessed my life. I have been given only the gifts of humility because I seek you for direction when I am feeling lost. I also have perseverance in not giving up on your love, even in dark and trying times. Let us not be filled by some, let us know for certain that your grace is available to all.

Let us believe, Oh Lord.

Amen

November 17

"The one who plants and the one who waters has one purpose, and they will each be rewarded according to their own labor." 1 Corinthians 5:13

Dear Lord,

I started some time ago on this journey of seeking you. My dedication has waxed and waned over the years, but your presence is a constant. I also surround myself with other seekers. We commune, as we share our blessings and ideas. Your love multiplies in shared experience.

It is never too late. Anyone may start to nurture the fruits of the spirit at any age. For me, it came to a certain point in my mid-30s where I was completely empty inside. I had nowhere to turn to get support. I had to start from that emptiness to rebuild and re-engage with you slowly, over time. You have renewed me. There are still ups and downs, however, I have resources to lift me up now.

Amen

November 18

"Each of you should give what you have decided in your heart to give, not reluctantly or under compulsion, for God loves a cheerful giver" 2 Corinthians 9:7

Dear Lord,

You have blessed me with life. In turn, I give back. In the past, I gave to the church. I search my heart deeply before giving. I give of my time, I give of my prayers. I give of my enrichment and support. I give financially to benevolent organizations.

Prior to giving, I consider the structure and mission of the organizations. Are the services provided in alignment with my own spiritual journey? If not, I listen to your call and donate accordingly. I continually take inventory of how I extend my resources. If one organization no longer works for my purposes, let me let go in love, and not become bitter.

It may seem difficult to find, but humankindness does exist. May I not become hard of heart.

Amen

November 19

"You have set our inequities before you our secret sins in the light of your presence" Psalm 90:8

Dear Lord,

Only you know my whole story. Only to you my life is an open book. You know where I excel and where I fall short. I have a tendency to want to hide my defects away from you and the world. I need to remember that you already know the open book of my life.

For only when I come before you and pour my whole heart out to you can your healing begin. You shine a light into my soul. Only in doing so can goodness be nurtured. In darkness, life decays and dies. May I seek nurturing and growth. May I be constantly willing to own my shortcomings, not only in privacy with you Lord, but also with my intimate friends.

Today I will accept myself as I am and I will invite you into a meaningful life experience with me.

Amen

November 20

"Brothers and sisters, if someone is caught in sin, you who live by the Spirit should restore that person gently. But watch yourselves, or you may be tempted." Galatians 6:1

Dear Lord,

When someone in my life is not making good choices, may I respond with kindness. May I not cast judgment. May I gently instruct for I would want the same treatment if I were engaging in sin. Each of us has our own vulnerabilities and our particular ways of veering off course.

May I practice detachment, however, may I learn how to love from a distance so that I myself do not become ensnared by bad choices. I am just as vulnerable as anyone else to giving in to temptation. May I also recognize attempts to glorify behavior that is not in keeping with what is best for my life.

Amen

November 21

"And let us consider how we may spur one another on toward love and good deeds." Hebrews 10:24

Dear Lord,

We are community-driven people. We thrive in tribes. We gain accountability in this way; we make ourselves known to each other. Teach us how to build up communities amongst ourselves that are based in love. We need to commune in unity, but also in a manner that honors uniqueness and individuality.

Condemnation, overbearing power plays, mind control and manipulation are not community-building elements. Such displays incite fear and mistrust. Perfection does not exist here among humans. Only you have been made perfect in love. May we emulate that. May we bring that to our group interactions to invite growth and peace.

Amen

November 22

"A generous person will prosper; whoever refreshes others will be refreshed." Proverbs 11:25

Dear Lord,

You instruct me to work, which brings blessings on me. In turn, I give of my means and my time. May we all be willing to do this. May we all be willing to participate in a culture with mutual give and take. May we be willing to give our surplus to those of our nation who are struggling.

I have heard it said that, "a chain is only as strong as its weakest link." Instead of our common practice of cutting off the weak links, may we provide care and understanding by nurturing the weak parts. I have myself found blessings in doing so. I seek your direction in regards to how to extend my resources.

Amen

November 23

"Command them to do good, to be rich in good deeds, and to be generous and willing to share." 1 Timothy 6:18

Dear Lord,

I was taught to share by my family. Bless my mom for her ways. May we practice that and may the practice be extended to those outside the family. I have built many relationships based on the sharing of my time and means. There are good people out there who want to help. There are also those in need who want to learn and grow.

May we be blessed with discernment in deciding with whom to share our means. We must be seekers. We must diligently pursue the path to your kingdom. The way is difficult. It is, however, worth it. I stumble daily along the way. I pick myself up, I dust myself off and I keep going.

Amen

November 24

"Into your hands I commit my spirit; deliver me, Lord my faithful God" Psalm 31:5

Dear Lord,

I am on a spiritual journey. I seek you each day. I allow you to direct my life and my path. Some days your direction is clear, some days I feel as though I am wandering in the wilderness. Regardless, I devote myself to the practice. I no longer fear you. I trust that you will hear my desperate cries.

You have delivered me from judgment. You invite me into a joyful community with you and with other like-minded folks. I have faith that you will not abandon me as long as I continue to pursue you and seek to listen to your voice, which quietly speaks. May I drown out the noise of the world. May I seek you in solitude and breathe life into that wounded space within me. Healing and wholeness are available when I allow them.

May I grant you permission to work in my life, today and every day.

Amen

November 25

"I myself am convinced, my brothers and sisters, that you yourselves are full of goodness, filled with knowledge and competent to instruct one another." Romans 15:14

Dear Lord,

We as spiritual beings are not meant to exist purely in isolation. You have designed us to grow in communion with one another. The modern Western experience of a faith community involves electing leaders to govern over the masses. May we all remember that no one spirit has more value than another. We are all equal in your eyes. All have a role to play.

May we be willing to set ego aside and listen to the voices of the marginalized. Some of our strongest and most dedicated followers have been shunned as they do not fit the prototype of the typical leader. All have gifts to bring. All can make a contribution and offer perspective. We can see each other's opportunities. Those who shut the door on growth shall wither and die.

May I always choose growth, Oh Lord.

Amen

November 26

"'But love your enemies, do good to them, and lend to them without expecting to get anything back. Then your reward will be great, and you will be children of the Most High, because he is kind to the ungrateful and the wicked."
Luke 6:35

Dear Lord,

Please help me to practice grace today with humankind. Often I do not like how I am treated or what is going on in the world. I get a knee-jerk reaction to retaliate or hold a grudge. Please help me to be a free-flowing conduit of your love and kindness. As I know and understand, you love each and every one of us. You invite us into closer communion with you through spiritual growth.

Let me remember that it is not my place to punish or inflict consequences. I leave your communication with others up to you. But may I seek solace and pull closer to you when I am placed in harm's way. Those who fear you and resist you cannot move into that space.

May I also be willing to check myself, as sometimes the fault is mine.

Amen

November 27

"Let us not become weary in doing good, for at the proper time we will reap a harvest if we do not give up." Galatians 6:9

Dear Lord,

May I seek the Spirit through service. Your love connects us as one people. When I connect with others in this way, it benefits me as well. If I burn out on a service commitment, may I gracefully lay that task down and allow you to nurture me. In time, I can look for another way of giving. No one other than you can direct me as to where I am best utilized.

Saying no when asked is encouraged. If the time and place is not right for me to involve myself, may I allow myself to give voice to that. My ministry is my own. Whereas I may overlap with others from time to time, I need to seek direction in regards to how to involve myself from you and you alone.

May I work to strengthen my connection. May I hear your voice speak.

Amen

November 28

"They speak of the glorious splendor of your majesty — and I will meditate on your wonderful works." Psalm 145:5

Dear Lord,

You are well-loved among my friends and family. You have brought me into a community of genuine love and support and for this I'm grateful. You quell my fears and restore my hope in trying times. You come to me as a presence in solitude. You help carry the load and you comfort me.

I meditate on your Word and your ways daily. I am of limited human understanding. However, when my ego softens to allow it, you speak to me. You provide wisdom and guidance. You enlighten me at times and show me the way out of the darkness. May I be a beacon of light and truth to those who are still ensnared.

Your love is available to all. You reassure and you renew.

Amen

November 29

"but those who hope in the Lord will renew their strength. They will soar on wings like eagles; they will run and not grow weary, they will walk and not be faint." Isaiah 40:31

Dear Lord,

A faith practice has a waiting period. I was quite lost and struggling when embarking upon this journey. I have been warring over time with something I was taught as a child. I believed that you could only be experienced through an organized church. I believed that I needed others to help me to understand how to relate to you.

As I had been forced out of that model, I sought another way. As I have dedicated myself to this practice, I have been able to come into an experience of who you are. I have been able to develop a strong, personal relationship with you. This was not something that was taught to me in church.

You renew me; you strengthen me each day.

Amen

November 30

"My son, do not despise the Lord's discipline, and do not resent his rebuke, because the Lord disciplines those he loves," Proverbs 3:11

Dear Lord,

You parent me and you shepherd me. As an adult and as a parent, I often feel as though I make the rules. We all answer to you in the end. When I lay down to sleep at night and I am restless, I know that I have something on my heart that separates me from having a strong connection with you.

You do create consequences for me when I veer off course. When I am being corrected by you, it is often unpleasant. When I work to realign myself with the goodness of your ways, you inevitably restore me. Your forgiveness is bountiful. May I allow you to guide me and direct me today. May I not fall into ego or self-propulsion. May I accept correction and when it comes, may I learn from it and grow.

Amen

December 1

"Am I now trying to win the approval of human beings, or of God? Or am I trying to please people? If I were still trying to please people, I would not be a servant of Christ." Galatians 1:10

Dear Lord,

I worry way too much about how I will be perceived by others. My mind spins at times. I lose sleep. May I instead yoke myself only to you and to your ways. May I allow my community of like-minded fellows to build up a wall around me. May I let those with conflicted views fall to the wayside.

I cannot be everything to everyone. I know that that is not your intention for me. Not all of the people who I come into contact with are spiritually minded. Most are quite materialistic. So, whereas I do want to learn how to love them from from a distance, may I learn how to create safe space for myself to insulate and detach from those relationships when needed.

Thank you for hearing my heart today.

Amen

December 2

"give thanks in all circumstances; for this is God's will for you in Christ Jesus." 1 Thessalonians 5:18

Dear Lord,

You have richly blessed my life. I also carry a heavy load. I know you are with me every step of the way. Please forgive me for those times when I feel bitter, resentful or envious. It is easy to look at the exterior presentation of others lives and compare that to the intimate reality of my life.

Please help me to maintain an intimate circle with whom I can practice transparency, as this is where spiritual growth seems to flourish for me. Unfortunately the church communities in which I have had prior involvement were mostly not safe spaces for me to express myself in this way. I express my gratitude to you today that you are blessing me with an inner circle now where I can commune deeply. Please help me to use discernment regarding who to open up to. May others also be willing to open their hearts in return.

Amen

December 3

"In him we were also chosen, having been predestined according to the plan of him who works out everything in conformity with the purpose of his will" Ephesians 1:11

Dear Lord,

As I look back on my life, I see that there was a divine purpose in all that has transpired. I have traveled through some very dark times. I have gone to battle with my inner demons. I still fight them today. The pain and despair of these times has led me to seek you. It has drawn me into a very deep relationship with you.

I have also become a teacher of sorts to others who fight in this way. We commune together. We support each other. We bless each other's lives and encourage wholeness. There are times of excess and times to tighten our belts. There are times to celebrate and times to pray. There are times of communion and there are times for solitary reflection.

May I learn to regulate. May I not get too out of balance on the fulcrum of life.

Amen

December 4

"Give me a sign of your goddess, that my enemies may see it and be put to shame, for you, Lord, have helped me and comforted me." Psalm 86:17

Dear Lord,

Some of the people who are working the hardest against me are those closest to me. May I be discerning who I let into my inner circle. May I insulate myself from spiritual warfare as I build a fortress of like-minded folk who support me in my mission. Some of those in my life are well-meaning, but they rely too heavily on me, instead of on building and maintaining their own connection to you. Others hate me because of you.

May I resist the urge to draw near to those who are not in fit spiritual condition. May I instead gently instruct, amongst your disciples, a practice that leads to a deeper communion with you. May I not be shy about retreat. If how I carry your message is not being well-received, may I retreat into myself and redouble my efforts. I know that upon doing so I will emerge stronger and more capable.

Amen

December 5

"'If a kingdom is divided against itself, that kingdom cannot stand." Mark 3:24

Dear Lord,

I see two separate camps emerging in the world today. Your followers tear each other down and have no unity. I see too many political teachings being preached as doctrine. Your tender mercy is often reserved only for those in positions of power. Your work was with the lowly. Your work was with the marginalized.

Your church has mostly fallen into the hands of the Pharisees, who make laws that are difficult, if not impossible, to follow. The marginalized are becoming the majority. May the church be willing to reform. May the church be willing to be a peacemaker; to hear unique voices and experiences. If it does not, it seems as though it will not survive.

May we prioritize unity. May we seek out the commonalities, not the differences, among the body.

Amen

December 6

"And my God will meet all your needs according to the riches of his glory in Christ Jesus." Philippians 4:19

Dear Lord,

I have a lot of fears of scarcity. I worry there will not be enough food, enough time or enough money in my life. I have been known to hoard my resources in the past as result of being overcome by thoughts of not having enough. As I draw near to you, you reassure me that you will bless me abundantly.

I do not have an excess of provisions. I have what I need, however, and I have enough to be generous with my means. I practice giving back as I feel called. It is difficult not to fall into these concerns from time to time. When I do, instead of grasping and clinging to material possessions, I force myself to surrender and accumulate the gifts of your kingdom.

You do provide for me and for that I am grateful.

Amen

December 7

"You, God, are my God, earnestly I seek you; I thirst for you, my whole being longs for you, in a dry and parched land where there is no water." Psalm 63:1

Dear Lord,

I dedicate myself to you in prayer and devotion daily. These are times of famine and drought, both literally and figuratively, in the world. My soul thirsts for you and I long for meaning and answers to many questions. I do not get concrete answers most of the time. I get asked to make a leap of faith. I do this often and I am rewarded.

You are the living water, Lord. When I seek you first, you lead me to abundance. Oftentimes, doing so requires me to leave behind loved ones and sentimentalities which has been difficult. When I do so, however, you lead me to abundance.

This path is available to all who surrender to it.

Amen

December 8

"If we confess our sins, he is faithful and just and will forgive us our sins." 1 John 1:9

Dear Lord,

I come before you today and I lay my misdeeds, at your feet, I ask that you be present with me in my daily battle against self-centeredness, egotism, improper boundaries and greed. Please help me to keep you as sovereign over me as I go through this day. Bless me with humility. May I recognize temptation and all other impulses that are not of your godly kingdom.

I fall short in some way each day. I am imperfectly human. May I grow more in your likeness each day. However, when I overstep, may I be willing to accept corrections. I seek you in solitude each day. I open my heart to hear your voice. I renew myself in your love, Oh Lord.

My mind is clearer and my heart more open.

Amen

December 9

"Fear of man will prove to be a snare, but whoever trusts in the Lord is kept safe." Proverbs 29:25

Dear Lord,

May I be more genuine and authentic with others who travel with me. My tendency is to want to try to present an image of being pulled together. When I open myself up to vulnerability, some days I am a mess. May I not be afraid of others' opinions of me.

Through you, Lord, I am empowered. Whereas it may repel others at times when I break open, that can attract some who are heavy and weighted down. When I offer my mess to you, when I share myself with my community, I become whole through union with like-minded fellows. I know that safety is in your warm embrace and in communal love.

You give light and love, Oh Lord. You warm my heart.

Amen

December 10

"'But when he, the Spirit of truth, comes he will guide you into all the truth. He will not speak on his own; he will speak only what he hears, and he will tell you what is yet to come." John 16:13

Dear Lord,

As I draw nearer and nearer to you, you put me more in touch with your inner voice. I come more into contact with the Spirit which lies within. It is a still, small voice that speaks to me and guides me. It is an internal GPS of sorts that can be tapped into when I am lost and don't know where to turn.

I do not know what will happen in the future. I have an intuition that if I continue to stay tapped into your source power, that I will not be left behind. I need to remain willing to quiet myself each day; to give you my doubts, questions and cries to stay open to receiving.

Although I know that change is coming, I trust that you will care for me and that I have a purpose.

Amen

December 11

"For sin shall no longer be your master, because you are not under the law, but under grace." Romans 6:14

Dear Lord,

I draw nearer to you each day as I devote myself more and more to you. I am not a perfect person, as you know. I have my moments of weakness and I fall short, as all humans do. Your grace covers me, however, and brings me back into the light. I do not have to go deeper and deeper into darkness if I do not want to.

As I cleanse myself more and more of sin, I grow in your ways. I become more fortified in your love and I gain power through you when I work in harmony with you. My purpose becomes clearer. May I always be willing to allow you to lift me up after I stumble. May I not allow pride to keep me from owning my deeds, Oh Lord.

You are a good and gracious Lord whose forgiveness abounds.

Amen

December 12

"'I have the right to do anything.' you say–but not everything is beneficial. 'I have the right to do anything'–but I will not be mastered by anything." 1 Corinthians 6:12

Dear Lord,

You have blessed us with free will. Nothing inherently prevents me from seeking an ungodly path in life. As I have done so previously, I will say that the consequences of my actions have not always been positive. There are things that weighed on my conscience several years after the choice to act on instinct was made.

If I seek you first in all things; in all decisions, I have assurance that I will not give myself over to dark forces. As I strengthen my relationship with you, I can request your guidance and insight before committing to an action. I can check in with my conscience beforehand to see how the thought sits with me.

You provide wisdom and insight when I genuinely seek.

Amen

December 13

"A gossip betrays a confidence, but a trustworthy person keeps a secret." Proverbs 11:13

Dear Lord,

I have been on both sides of gossip. I have been betrayed by it, however, I have also participated in it. It is ugly on both sides. Sometimes we are open to hearing the deep truths of the pain of others. Sometimes we need to put our energy into carrying our own loads. May we learn to accept ourselves regardless of the situation and act accordingly.

May I learn to seek you in silence, when I am feeling overwhelmed or out of control. I do not always have the answers. I do not always know why people do what they do. Today I give myself permission to stay in the dark until someone directly makes something my business.

May I learn to give others a sacred silence when needed and may I learn to seize that for myself as well.

Amen

December 14

"'Blessed are those who are poor in spirit, for theirs is the kingdom of heaven." Matthew 5:3

Dear Lord,

Please help me not to get caught up in false pride or egocentric thinking. Sometimes I am received by others as though I know something, or have some coveted information. I am a disciple just as any follower. I study a lot to satisfy my own curiosity, however, each day one of us should seek in our own way for answers which resonate with us.

If we diligently devote ourselves to you and seek, we will find our way. We will meet fellow travelers who are of the same tribe. We will form our own personal relationship with you so that we become more unwavering. It is only in the maintaining of humility and in constantly remaining teachable that we can continually renew and grow our faith.

May I always keep my heart open, to embrace new ways of understanding.

Amen

December 15

"But avoid foolish controversies and genealogies and arguments and quarrels about the law, because these are unprofitable and useless." Titus 3:9

Dear Lord,

It seems as though we spend so much time arguing with each other as Christians over things that are very trivial. We have so many different camps or sects that we are not a unified body. This makes us vulnerable and weak. We divide ourselves politically and technically.

May we seek to be a unified body in your name. May we keep genuine love as your first commandment. May we be inclusive, not exclusive. May we treasure our differences instead of being threatened by them. Only if we are willing to practice these principles can we collectively gain the power to win souls in your name. If we cannot, we are no different than any secular organization.

May we realign ourselves as one body in your name.

Amen

December 16

"This is why, for Christ's sake, I delight in weaknesses, insults, in hardships, in persecutions, difficulties. For when I am weak, I am strong." 2 Corinthians 12:10

Dear Lord,

I am not a masochist. I do not take on torture for no reason. I stand with what I believe in, to the best of my abilities and absorb the world's reaction. Sometimes, as I walk down the street, I sense our community looking on with charity. Please give me the strength to hold firm in what I believe and not to allow loneliness and self-pity to make me want to run away.

Many times I look around with a heavy heart as others seem to be celebrating. As I continue to shoulder my burdens, I grow stronger each day in the Spirit. The more I become transparent about my difficulties, the easier it is to also maintain an attitude of gratitude. This I find as contagious as others seek me out.

May we not be afraid to expose our struggles so that we may gain strength.

Amen

December 17

"Jesus went through all the towns and villages, teaching in the synagogues, proclaiming the good news of the kingdom and healing every disease and sickness." Matthew 9:35

Dear Lord,

May I not become discouraged by my unanswered pleas for you to cure hopeless illness. When confronted with the thought of your people, hopelessly suffering with many diseases, may we not lose faith. As I progress in age along this journey of life, I experience a number in my community with various illnesses, many of which are incurable.

What you can heal, Oh Lord, is sickness of the soul. Although we or our loved ones may become sick, it is possible to maintain healthy attitudes which have been known to prolong longevity and improve quality of life. What you can heal also are relationships. We can invite your love into our relationships at any time. Although certain individuals may not reciprocate, there is goodness Lord.

May all who seek find.

Amen

December 18

"Why, my soul, are you downcast? Why so disturbed within me? Put your hope in God, for I will yet praise him, my Savior and my God." Psalm 42:5

Dear Lord,

How many nights have I lost sleep? How many nights have I been disturbed by a mind that will not shut down? Other times I have been awakened in the middle of the night, fretting from troublesome dreams. When I have something on my conscience, a misdeed, it is difficult to find rest. When I am not reconciled wholly to you, I am blocked from deep and restful slumber.

It may be that I have harmed someone, either intentionally or unintentionally. It may be that I need to pray and seek your guidance on how to make restitution. It could be that I am trying to control, that I am not trusting you in some area of my life. I may be thinking I am being punished, instead of opening myself up to the many possibilities that avail themselves.

The comfort is there, sometimes it takes me several days or longer to find it. May I never stop searching.

Amen

December 19

"Surely the lowborn are but a breath, the highborn are but a lie. If weighted on a balance, they are nothing; together they are both only one breath." Psalm 62:9

Dear Lord,

As we struggle through life, we may think we are better than others as we have more. On the other hand, we may think that we are less than because we lack. The human experience is universal. All of life is but a vapor. We have a tiny slice of time here. We can choose to follow in your ways or we can get caught up in the tit for tat of the world. All struggle. Some may hide it better than others.

True love is born of genuine human connection. When we reveal ourselves, we invite support to cheer us on the narrow road. I am not fine. I am not OK. I am a real person who is really struggling. As I let go of the blaming and step into the pain of my own experience, I can invite healing and growth. Hopefully in doing so I can avoid being pulled off course.

Amen

December 20

"Be on guard; stand firm in the faith; be courageous; be strong." 1 Corinthians 16:13

Dear Lord,

May I keep a careful eye on who I allow myself to become close to. May I always value myself as a creature of your kingdom. May I see myself as someone worthy of your love, despite my misdeeds. May I seek to be close to only those who also seek growth and divine love. May I learn to instruct in your ways, but also keep a distance when needed. There is good in all people. It needs to be tenderly nurtured but it is very painful to let love in.

It is painful to admit the need. It is painful to reveal the pain of mistakes made, of needing others for direction, of not having all the answers. I do not have all the answers. I study a lot but sometimes my human mind does not piece things together in a way that is of your kingdom. I need feedback. People need people. May I find the community that you have designed for me, and seek to add to the fold.

Amen

December 21

"'Do not be like them, for your Father knows what you need before you ask him.'" Matthew 6:8

Dear Lord,

Although I may fret over some of my life circumstances, you know the needs of my heart. I am human. I plan out how I want my life to be, and when the reality differs from my desires, I sometimes become bitter or feel slighted. May I be able to practice acceptance. May I understand that, despite the hardship and pain that I endure, you know exactly what I need to happen in my life to develop character.

I do have a tendency to want to come to you in prayer and plead with you to remove certain situations. Health problems are difficult. Parenting is difficult. Relationships are difficult. It is easy for me to blame my unhappiness on these circumstances. It is easy for me to feel as though I would be in good spirits if only…if only you would remove this from my life. If only you would remove that.

The truth is, Lord, when I am rightly connected to you, I can endure and accept my life as is.

Amen

December 22

"Therefore my heart is glad and my tongue rejoices; my body also will rest secure." Psalm 16:9

Dear Lord,

I work daily to nurture my connection with you. When I am out of alignment with your kingdom, I seek to find how to right my wrongs. As we struggle through our human condition, there is a lot of gray area. We may seek council and still not receive closure on complicated involvements. We may find peace momentarily, only to find ourselves out of balance a few days or weeks later.

When I am in right alignment with your kingdom, I feel a peace in my soul. I feel your divine protection and guidance sheltering me from the difficulties of life. My struggles do not disappear, but my load is lightened. I can find the commonality in the human experience. I can enjoy my relationships and share laughter and connection, in spite of my troubles.

Your presence in my life is a treasure that I do not want to lose.

Amen

December 23

"praise be to the God and Father of our Lord Jesus Christ, the Father of compassion and the God of comfort, who comforts us in all our troubles, so that we can comfort those in any trouble with the comfort we ourselves have received from God." 2 Corinthians 1:3-4

Dear Lord,

As I come to you each day, wholly broken and incapable when left to my own devices, you comfort and strengthen me. I, who was once downtrodden, have been lifted up, according to your grace. I have seen many others restored to wholeness through your comfort and community as well. You ask very little in return.

We are instructed to bring the message of your grace to others who suffer in kind. There is a tiny ray of light in any darkness. Even if we cannot see it, if we make the leap of faith, and do the work to seek, we will inevitably find it. Your love is best expressed in community. Love was shown to me, more so than told me to. Love is an action verb.

May I learn how to effectively love those in need. May I make a relevant contribution to the world today.

Amen

December 24

"So Joseph also went up from the town of Nazareth in Galilee to Judea, to Bethlehem the town of David, because he belonged to the house of David." Luke 2:4

Dear Lord,

When I am in tune with you, I hear your voice. I experience things in synchronicity as my internal GPS directs me where you call me. You do have a purpose for us. I do feel a calling. I was so lost at one point, at several points, Lord. I have thought many times of taking my own life. Something kept me hanging on. I was asked to make a leap of faith and to diligently seek to do the work you requested.

I did not always do the right things. At different times we are all more in tune with our divine calling than at others. I don't know of anyone who never made a choice they regretted, or who didn't look back and think that some things could have worked out better. Some are more in tune than others. Some are born and asked by you to help lead. Things happened in the world just the way they needed to for your message to be made available.

May I do my best to communicate my understanding.

Amen

December 25

"But the angel said to them, 'Do not be afraid. I will bring you good news that will cause great joy for all the people. Today in the town of David a Savior has been born to you; he is the Messiah, the Lord.'" Luke 2:10-11

Dear Lord,

Regardless of where I am spiritually speaking, I can always be grateful to be a part of your love. I am in awe that you have come, your living Spirit, to call me out of darkness and realign me with your goodness. At this time may we remember the gift of your presence and how you came to bring light to our lost and lonely world.

May we remember to celebrate the peace you represented. May we shift our focus from the material to the spiritual and community, which is where you remain eternal. I pray that I will be willing to step into the light of your love. I pray that I may be willing to leave behind my transgressions as well and to commune with you in grace and truth.

Amen

December 26

"And the child grew and became strong; he was filled with wisdom, and the grace of God was on him." Luke 2:40

Dear Lord,

You certainly fulfilled your purpose here on Earth. You studied and devoted yourself wholly to Father. The message of your Word and wisdom lives in our lives and hearts eons later. May we learn from your example. May we be peaceful warriors who find our unity with you in loving fellowship with each other.

May we come together to pray and break bread. May our mission be as yours was, to "seek and save the lost." May we love not only our like-minded fellows, but also our enemies and others with challenging personalities. May we constantly be willing to practice self-evaluation and to need criticism for it is only in doing so that we enlarge and diversify our faith fellowship.

We praise you for an example of a life well lived.

Amen

December 27

"The righteous cry out, and the Lord hears them; he delivers them from all their troubles." Psalm 34:17

Dear Lord,

So many times I come to pray with a heavy heart. Sometimes I don't even know what to say in my prayers. If I sincerely open my heart, however, you enter. Sometimes there are no words, only silent sincerity and emotion; sometimes only tears are a way of sharing. You hear me and you comfort me as a trusted friend. May I treasure that. May I never forget that you avail yourself to us in this way.

As I surrender and release to you, you strengthen me. The light inside my soul grows brighter, even though my heart is breaking. You break me open. You bond me to you and to my like- minded fellows. You have given me the gift of life. May I give and genuinely receive in return.

Amen

December 28

"Very early in the morning, while it was still dark, Jesus got up, and went off to a solitary place, where he prayed." Mark 1:35

Dear Lord,

As I retreat daily into the sanctity of my safe space, I find you in solitude. I seek you privately and silently. As I continue to carve out time away from the chronic noise of our modern era, you speak to me and you listen. Over time your message becomes clearer. I turn to you as I start to get a headache; when I become overwhelmingly exhausted and detached from what is going on around me.

You refresh me. You renew me. You direct me to the next right action. Over time you provide purpose and direction. You clear my mind and restore mental clarity. If I have learned one thing, it is that I cannot stray from giving time with you top priority.

The world would be a kinder, gentler place if we could all do as outlined above.

Amen

December 29

"'What good is it for someone to gain the whole world, yet forfeit their soul?'" Mark 8:36

Dear Lord,

In our Western world, wealth and status have become the focus of our world. This is a dead end road. How disappointing it would be to get to the end of our life's journey and find ourselves lost and alone. May I always remember to take time for you each day and to let everything else fall into place in my life around that.

If relationships do not support that, may I detach from them. May I fill my inner circle with like-minded folk, not those who will pull me off course. May I seek out career opportunities that allow me time and space to put my relationship with you first.

May I seek direction from you. Whisper softly to my soul in your still, small voice.

Amen

December 30

"God looks down from heaven on all mankind to see if there are any who understand, any who seek God." Psalm 53:2

Dear Lord,

Once my heart was closed to you. I was stubborn and prideful. I thought I could handle life on my own. I have proven this to be incorrect on more than one account. As I carve out time to diligently seek you, your purpose for my life becomes clearer. May I always remember to make this time for you.

Life is challenging. At times I have thought I could turn to the government, the media, church, higher education or other institutions for direction. It turns out that in the end, the path to higher understanding comes only from deepening my relationship with you. May I remember to devote time to that daily. If I get off course, may I remember that devotion can begin at any time. May I seek to move closer to you, not turn away.

Amen

December 31

"'For I know the plans I have for you,' declares the Lord, plans to prosper you and not to harm you, plans to give you hope and a future.'" Jeremiah 29:11

Dear Lord,

Life is a journey in and out of many different social constructs. Disconnecting from a core belief or community can be painful, overwhelming and confusing. May we give ourselves the time and space to grieve. Throughout my own personal journey, I have chosen to step out of my cocoon and to build anew.

From each group or system, I have uncovered truths about myself. I seek now to treasure those experiences and to build something whole and unique to myself. I look forward to sharing that with others and celebrating others who have transcended their mental constructs and found an identity for themselves that honors their personal truth, whatever that may be.

Amen

ABOOKS

ALIVE Book Publishing and ALIVE Publishing Group
are imprints of Advanced Publishing LLC,
3200 A Danville Blvd., Suite 204, Alamo, California 94507

Telephone: 925.837.7303
alivebookpublishing.com